MW00897111

The Essential
Mediterranean Diet
Cookbook For Beginners 2024

**2000 Days of Creative, Tasty and Easy Mediterranean
Recipes for a Happier and Healthier life
(Incl. 30 day meal plan &shopping list)**

Sophia Wilson

Copyright © 2024 by - Sophia Wilson - All Rights Reserved

This book is jointly owned by the author and the publisher and is protected by copyright laws. No part of this e-book may be reproduced, distributed, modified, or used for commercial purposes without the prior written permission of both the author and the publisher. For any quotation or reprint, please contact the author or the publisher for authorization.

Legal Notice

The recipes provided in this book are for reference and personal use only. The author and the publisher make no warranties regarding the accuracy, safety, or suitability of the recipes. Readers should use these recipes at their own risk and comply with appropriate food safety and hygiene regulations. Efforts have been made to ensure that the information in this book is accurate and complete. However, due to the rapidly changing nature of science and research, the author and the publisher do not warrant the accuracy of the information, text, and graphics contained within the book.

Note on Disclaimer

The recipes in this book may contain personal preferences and taste biases. Readers should make appropriate adjustments to these recipes based on their own health conditions, food allergies, and personal needs. The author and the publisher are not liable for any consequences resulting from the use of these recipes.

The author is not a licensed practitioner, physician or medical professional and offers no medical treatment, diagnoses, suggestions or counselling. The information presented herein has not been evaluated by the U.S Food & Drug Administration, and it is not intended to diagnose, treat, cure or prevent any disease. Full medical clearance from a licensed physician should be obtained before beginning or modifying any diet, exercise or lifestyle program, and physician should be informed of all nutritional changes. The author claims no responsibility to any person or entity for any liability, loss, damage or death caused or alleged to be caused directly or indirectly as a result of the use, application or interpretation of the information presented herein.

TABLE OF CONTENT

INTRODUCTION

The Mediterranean diet has its roots in the culinary traditions of the countries bordering the Mediterranean Sea, such as Italy, Greece, Spain, and others. This diet emerged from the natural resources and agricultural practices of these regions.

For centuries, the people in these areas relied on local, fresh produce. The warm climate was conducive to growing a wide variety of fruits, vegetables, grains, and olives. Seafood was readily available due to the proximity to the sea.

The culture surrounding the Mediterranean diet is deeply intertwined with family and social gatherings. Meals are often long and communal, with an emphasis on sharing and enjoying food together. It's not just about nourishment but also about connection and celebration.

The use of olive oil, a staple in Mediterranean cooking, has historical significance. It was not only for its taste but also for its health benefits.

Wine is also a common element in Mediterranean culture, often consumed in moderation with meals.

The Mediterranean diet reflects the values of simplicity, seasonality, and a connection to the land and sea.

CHAPTER 1

What exactly is the Mediterranean diet?

Essentially, adhering to a Mediterranean diet implies consuming food in the manner traditionally followed by people in the Mediterranean region. Of course, not all individuals in the Mediterranean region have the same eating habits. Thus, the Mediterranean dietary pattern is intended to serve as a general guideline for a healthy and diverse diet that gives priority to plant-based foods.

A Mediterranean diet is an eating approach that emphasizes fruits, vegetables, legumes, and whole grains. Compared to a typical Western diet, it contains fewer ultra-processed foods and less meat. Doctors might suggest a Mediterranean diet to aid in disease prevention and maintaining people's health over a longer period. The Mediterranean region boasts various types of foods and cuisines, so there isn't a specific Mediterranean diet but rather a style of eating.

The Mediterranean diet places greater emphasis on plant foods than numerous other diets. Foods such as fruits, vegetables, whole grains, and legumes are the main components in meals and snacks. Meals might

incorporate small quantities of fish, meat, or eggs. People frequently cook with olive oil and add herbs and spices to enhance the flavor.

Benefits of the Mediterranean Diet

The advantages of the Mediterranean diet are widely recognized. Here are some key benefits:

1. **Enhances cardiovascular health:** The Mediterranean diet highlights the utilization of olive oil as the main fat source, and the monounsaturated fatty acids in olive oil can assist in lowering cholesterol levels and minimizing the risk of cardiovascular disorders.

2. **Offers abundant antioxidants:** Fruits, vegetables, and nuts in the Mediterranean diet are abundant in antioxidants like vitamin C, vitamin E, and polyphenols, which can aid in reducing oxidative damage and safeguarding cells from harm.

3. **Decreases the risk of chronic diseases:** The Mediterranean diet is linked to a decreased likelihood of obesity, type 2 diabetes, specific cancers, and Alzheimer's disease.

4. **Supplies balanced nutrition:** The Mediterranean diet emphasizes a variety of food choices, encompassing vegetables, fruits, whole grains, legumes, fish, and nuts, providing a rich source of vitamins, minerals, and fiber that contribute to overall well-being.

5. **Benefits mental health:** The social aspect of the Mediterranean diet and its cultural tradition of relishing food are associated with mental wellness. Sharing meals with family and friends and enjoying food at a leisurely pace can bring about contentment and happiness.

In conclusion, the Mediterranean diet, characterized by its plethora of plant-based foods, moderate consumption of animal-based foods, use of olive oil, and emphasis on social dining, is regarded as a healthy dietary pattern associated with cardiovascular health, antioxidant effects, reduced risk of chronic diseases, and enhanced mental well-being.

Principles of the Mediterranean Diet

The main principle of the Mediterranean diet is to focus on whole, unprocessed foods and to embrace a lifestyle that incorporates regular physical activity, sufficient hydration, and conscious eating habits.

1. **Diverse plant-based foods:** The Mediterranean diet highlights the consumption of a wide range of fruits, vegetables, whole grains, legumes, and nuts to obtain various nutrients and fiber.

2. **Moderate intake of animal-based foods:** The Mediterranean diet stresses consuming fish, poultry, and dairy products moderately as sources of high-quality protein and essential fatty acids.

3. **Use of olive oil as the main source of fat:** Olive oil, which is rich in monounsaturated fatty acids, is beneficial for cardiovascular health.

4. **Moderate alcohol consumption:** Mainly red wine, moderate alcohol intake can facilitate socialization and relaxation.

5. **Social dining and enjoyment of food:** The Mediterranean diet underlines sharing meals with family and friends, relishing food slowly, and enhancing social interaction and satisfaction.

Can the Mediterranean Diet Lead to Weight Loss?

The Mediterranean diet, as a traditional eating pattern for many cultures worldwide, wasn't originally intended for weight loss. However, it turns out that this one of the healthiest diets globally is also beneficial for maintaining a proper weight.

One review examined five trials involving overweight and obese individuals and discovered that after one year, those adhering to a Mediterranean diet lost up to 11 pounds (lb) more than those following a low-fat diet. But the same study found comparable weight loss in other diets, such as low-carb diets and the American Diabetes Association diet. The researchers suggest that the results imply that "there is no perfect diet for achieving sustained weight loss in overweight or obese individuals."

Yet, the Mediterranean diet can be a diverse and inclusive approach to losing weight, which avoids tricks and doesn't require calorie or macronutrient counting like some other diets (for example, the Ketogenic diet). Moreover, with its emphasis on healthy fats, it is also satisfying. That being said, in 2022, U.S. News & World Report ranked the Mediterranean diet as No. 1 in the category of Best Diets Overall and 12 in its list of Best Weight-Loss Diets.

Researchers note that it's not a guaranteed success and instead depends on how you consume. Portion sizes and the amount of fat matter even in healthy diets like the Mediterranean.

The crux of the Mediterranean diet lies in "Moderation"

Everything is permitted in the Mediterranean Diet, even cake. But only in a moderate amount. The people in this region comprehend that an excessive amount of a good thing is detrimental to their health. This encompasses the good foods as well. Consuming too many calories leads to weight gain and diseases, even if those calories originate from healthy foods.

It is essential to bear in mind that the Mediterranean diet is not a one-size-fits-all solution, and portion sizes as well as the overall calorie intake should be customized to individual goals and requirements. Consulting a healthcare professional or a registered dietitian can offer personalized directions for integrating these foods into a balanced diet.

Mediterranean diet recommendations

1. **Increase plant consumption:** The Mediterranean diet suggests having more fruits, vegetables, whole grains, legumes, and nuts. These foods are abundant in vitamins, minerals, and fiber, which contribute to a healthy and balanced diet.

2. **Opt for fresh and seasonal produce:** The Mediterranean diet encourages the selection of fresh and seasonal ingredients. This guarantees the freshness and nutritional value of the food and offers the best flavors.

3. **Select whole grains:** The Mediterranean diet recommends choosing whole grains like whole wheat bread, brown rice, and whole wheat pasta. Whole grains are rich in dietary fiber, vitamins, and minerals, which facilitate digestion and help maintain stable blood sugar levels.

4. **Indulge in healthy fats:** The Mediterranean diet promotes the consumption of healthy fats such as olive oil, nuts, and avocados. These fats contain monounsaturated and polyunsaturated fatty acids, which are beneficial for cardiovascular health.

5. **Have fish twice a week:** The Mediterranean diet suggests consuming fish at least twice a week, like salmon, cod, and sardines. Fish is a good source of high-quality protein and omega-3 fatty acids, which are beneficial for heart health.

6. **Prepare vegetarian meals twice a week:** The Mediterranean diet proposes cooking vegetarian meals at least twice a week. Vegetarian meals can enhance the intake of vegetables and legumes, providing a rich source of nutrients and fiber.

7. **Consume cheese and yogurt moderately:** The Mediterranean diet advises having cheese and yogurt in moderation. These dairy products are rich in calcium and protein, but it is crucial to consume them in appropriate amounts.

8. **Restrict red meat intake:** The Mediterranean diet recommends limiting the consumption of red meat. It is suggested to choose more fish, poultry, and legumes as protein sources and reduce the intake of red meat.

9. **Enjoy a glass of wine moderately:** The Mediterranean diet suggests having a glass of wine in moderation. Moderate consumption of red wine can be beneficial for cardiovascular health, but it is important to control the intake.

Beneficial and Restricted Foods of the Mediterranean Diet

Foods to emphasize in the Mediterranean diet:

- **Fresh vegetables:** Vegetables form a fundamental part of the Mediterranean diet, offering essential vitamins, minerals, and fiber. Commonly consumed vegetables in this diet comprise tomatoes, cucumbers, eggplants, peppers, and leafy greens.
- **Seasonal fruits:** Fruits are also a significant element of the Mediterranean diet, providing natural sweetness and antioxidants. Popular fruits within the diet include oranges, lemons, grapes, pomegranates, and figs.
- **Oily fish:** Fish serves as a major protein source in the Mediterranean diet, and oily fish like salmon, sardines, and mackerel are rich in heart-healthy omega-3 fatty acids.
- **Chicken and poultry:** While red meat is restricted in the Mediterranean diet, chicken and other poultry constitute a good source of lean protein.
- **Olive oil:** Olive oil is a crucial component of the Mediterranean diet, providing healthy monounsaturated fats and antioxidants. It is utilized for cooking, dressing salads, and for bread dipping.
- **Red wine:** Red wine is consumed moderately in the Mediterranean diet and has been linked to a decreased risk of heart disease due to its antioxidant properties.

- **Whole grains:** Whole grains such as whole wheat, brown rice, and oats are a good source of fiber and nutrients and are a staple in the Mediterranean diet.
- **Nuts and seeds:** Nuts and seeds are a good source of healthy fats, protein, and fiber. Popular options include almonds, walnuts, pistachios, and sesame seeds.
- **Legumes:** Legumes such as chickpeas, lentils, and beans are a good source of protein, fiber, and nutrients and are a staple in the Mediterranean diet.
- **Greek yogurt:** Greek yogurt is a favored dairy product in the Mediterranean diet, providing protein and probiotics.
- **Cheese:** Cheese is consumed moderately in the Mediterranean diet and offers calcium and protein. Popular choices encompass feta, goat cheese, and Parmesan.
- **Garlic:** Garlic is a common flavoring agent in the Mediterranean diet and has been associated with various health benefits, including reducing inflammation and improving heart health.
- **Fresh herbs:** Fresh herbs such as basil, oregano, and thyme are employed to add flavor to dishes in the Mediterranean diet and provide antioxidants and other beneficial compounds.

Please be aware that these foods should be consumed moderately, taking into account individual nutritional needs and health conditions.

The Mediterranean diet demands restricted foods:

- **Refined carbohydrates:** These encompass processed foods such as white flour, white rice, candy, and pastries. These foods can rapidly elevate blood sugar levels and lack nutritional value.
- **Red meat:** Refers to beef, pork, lamb, and other such meats. Red meat is high in saturated fat and cholesterol, and excessive consumption is associated with cardiovascular disease and other health issues.
- **Processed meats:** Such as sausages, lunch meats, ham, etc. These foods typically contain high amounts of salt, fat, and additives, which increase the risk of chronic diseases.
- **High-sugar foods and beverages:** Such as candy, desserts, soft drinks, etc. Excessive sugar intake can result in weight gain, blood sugar fluctuations, and dental problems.
- **High-salt foods:** Including processed foods, pickled products, and high-salt seasonings. High salt intake might raise the risk of hypertension and cardiovascular disease.
- **High-saturated fat foods:** Such as butter, cream, full-fat dairy products, etc. These foods contain high levels of saturated fat, which may not be beneficial for heart health when consumed excessively.
- **Excessive alcohol:** Moderate consumption of red wine in the Mediterranean diet is beneficial for health, but excessive alcohol intake may have adverse effects on health, including liver damage and other health problems.
- **Refined seed oils:** Refers to refined vegetable oils such as soybean oil, corn oil, sunflower seed oil, etc. These oils are usually high in unhealthy fatty acids, and it is recommended to select healthier alternatives like olive oil.

In the Mediterranean diet, limiting the intake of these foods moderately and choosing healthier options can assist in maintaining a healthy lifestyle.

MEDITERRANEAN DIET PYRAMID

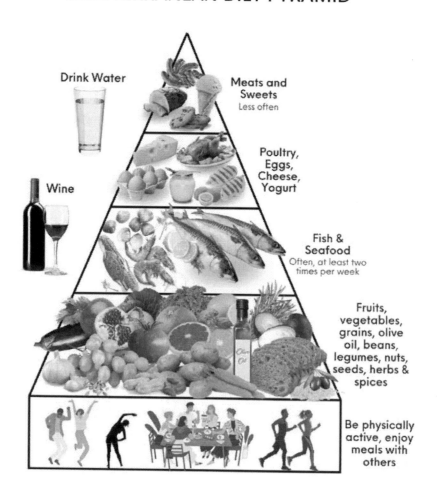

Drink Water

Meats and Sweets
Less often

Poultry, Eggs, Cheese, Yogurt

Wine

Fish & Seafood
Often, at least two times per week

Fruits, vegetables, grains, olive oil, beans, legumes, nuts, seeds, herbs & spices

Be physically active, enjoy meals with others

30-Day Meal Plan

Days	Breakfast	Lunch	Dinner	Snack/Dessert
1	Raspberries - Granola / P11	Asparagus Baked Plaice / P23	Spinach Orzo Soup / P46	Yogurt-Topped Squash Fritters / P70
2	Ciabatta With Fried Tomatoes / P10	Vegetable & Herb Chicken Cacciatore / P26	Seafood Risotto / P37	Turkish Stuffed Apricots With Rose Water And Pistachios / P74
3	Frittata / P14	Pan-Roasted Sea Bass With Wild Mushrooms / P18	White Gazpacho / P42	Classic Hummus / P68
4	Fresh Fruit And Plain Yogurt / P13	Broiled Bluefish With Preserved Lemon And Zhoug / P17	Whole-Wheat Spaghetti With Lentils, Pancetta, And Escarole / P35	Marinated Artichokes / P69
5	Ricotta Fig Oatmeal / P14	Chorizo Fish Stew / P22	Croatian Double-Crusted Vegetable Tart / P54	Lemon Ice / P77
6	Fried Cheese Toast / P13	Grilled Lamb Shish Kebabs / P29	Creamy Green Pea Pasta / P33	Spiced Biscotti / P75
7	White Bread With Shrimp And Dill Spread / P9	Pan-Seared Chicken Breasts With Chickpea Salad / P25	Roasted Mushrooms With Parmesan And Pine Nuts / P52	Creamy Turkish Nut Dip / P71
8	Fried Egg In a Bed Of Vegetables / P14	Red Wine Braised Beef Stew / P45	Moroccan-Style Carrot Salad / P59	Lemon Sherbet / P76
9	Cream Cheese Bread With Vegetables / P11	Greek-Style Braised Pork With Leeks / P30	Olive Oil Lemon Broiled Cod / P21	Zesty White Wine Marinated Olives / P70
10	Eggplant Spread / P12	Paprika Stewed Lamb / P43	Grilled Salmon Bulgur Salad / P63	Toasted Bread For Bruschetta / P71
11	Rye Pancakes With Green Onion Sauce And Red Caviar / P13	Za'Atar-Rubbed Butterflied Chicken / P27	Roasted Broccoli Salad / P62	Muhammara / P68
12	Hot Sandwiches With Cheese, Tomatoes And Greens / P9	Swordfish En Cocotte With Shallots, Cucumber, And Mint / P20	Couscous With Lamb, Chickpeas, And Orange / P38	Egg And Lime Cream / P77
13	Fried Ham Eggs / P12	Catalan Braised Rabbit / P30	Stuffed Bell Peppers With Spiced Beef, Currants, And Feta / P50	Olive-Stuffed Chicken Breasts / P71
14	Almond Mascarpone Dumplings / P15	Grilled Salmon With Butternut Squash Puree / P22	French Lentils With Carrots And Parsley / P39	Strawberries With Balsamic Vinegar / P74
15	Vegetable Frittata / P12	Honey Roasted Chicken With Rosemary Potatoes / P31	Mediterranean Quinoa Salad / P65	Olive Oil–Yogurt Cake / P75

16	Crab Donuts / P10	Penne And Fresh Tomato Sauce With Spinach And Feta / P33	Mediterranean-Style Tuna Salad / P60	Dark Chocolate Hazelnut Truffles / P76
17	Fresh Fruit And Plain Yogurt / P13	Grilled Pesto Salmon / P22	Stuffed Eggplants / P56	Peach Cobbler With a Twist / P79
18	Fried Egg In a Bed Of Vegetables / P14	Chicken Tagine With Chickpeas And Apricots / P28	Red Wine Braised Beef Stew / P45	Wild Berries With Ice / P79
19	Fried Cheese Toast / P13	Fig Lamb Stew / P46	Yogurt Romaine Salad / P63	Mussels Escabèche / P69
20	Raspberries - Granola / P11	Sicilian Fish Stew / P18	Grilled Zucchini And Red Onion With Lemon-Basil Dressing / P54	Classic Hummus / P68
21	Raspberries - Granola / P11	Fried Chicken With Tzatziki Sauce / P30	Bulgur Salad With Carrots And Almonds / P39	Creamy Turkish Nut Dip / P71
22	Ricotta Fig Oatmeal / P14	Spice Crusted Lamb Chops / P26	Spanish-Style Lentil And Chorizo Soup / P44	Turkish Stuffed Apricots With Rose Water And Pistachios / P74
23	Rye Pancakes With Green Onion Sauce And Red Caviar / P13	Zesty, Lettuce-Wrapped Chicken Gyros / P25	Creamy Parmesan Polenta / P34	Marinated Artichokes / P69
24	Eggplant Spread / P12	Calamari Stew With Garlic And Tomatoes / P19	Mediterranean Potato Salad / P64	Yogurt-Topped Squash Fritters / P70
25	Crab Donuts / P10	Herbed Lamb Cutlets With Roasted Vegetables / P27	One-Pot Curried Halloumi / P53	Spiced Biscotti / P75
26	Hot Sandwiches With Cheese, Tomatoes And Greens / P9	Seared Scallops With Orange-Lime Dressing / P19	Smoky Eggplant Balsamic Salad / P63	Olive Oil–Yogurt Cake / P75
27	Almond Mascarpone Dumplings / P15	Raisin Stuffed Lamb / P28	Spaghetti With Clams And Roasted Tomatoes / P36	Lemon Ice / P77
28	Frittata / P14	Braised Halibut With Leeks And Mustard / P17	Mediterranean Sausage Soup / P42	Peach Cobbler With a Twist / P79
29	Ciabatta With Fried Tomatoes / P10	Orzo With Greek Sausage And Spiced Yogurt / P34	Grilled Chicken Salad / P61	Dark Chocolate Hazelnut Truffles / P76
30	Cream Cheese Bread With Vegetables / P11	Healthy Tuna & Bean Wraps / P20	Italian Bean & Cabbage Soup / P45	Egg And Lime Cream / P77

CHAPTER 2: BREAKFAST

WHITE BREAD WITH SHRIMP AND DILL SPREAD

INGREDIENTS FOR 2 SERVINGS:

- salt and pepper
- 2 slices of white bread without crust (tramezzini bread)
- 80-100 g of pickled shrimp
- Tabasco sauce / 1 tbsp. sour cream
- 1 tbsp. chopped dill

DIRECTIONS:

1. Mix the dill with the sour cream and season with salt, pepper and tabasco sauce.
2. Drain the shrimp and mix with the dill spread.
3. Smear the spread on one slice of bread and cover with the other slice. Divide the bread diagonally and serve.

HOT SANDWICHES WITH CHEESE, TOMATOES AND GREENS

INGREDIENTS FOR 4 SERVINGS:

- 4 White bread
- 1 Green onion, bundle
- 1 Tomato
- 4 tbsp. White cheese
- 2 tsp. Butter
- 1 Parsley, bundle

DIRECTIONS:

1. Dry the slices of bread. Chop green onions and parsley.
2. Cheese mixed with butter, onions, and herbs.
3. Put the finished curd on the bread. Put thin slices of tomato on top.
4. Bake sandwiches in the microwave at full power for 2-3 minutes.

CRAB DONUTS

🦀 INGREDIENTS FOR 4 SERVINGS:

- parsley
- 250 g small crabs in the shell
- oil
- 250 g flour
- salt
- 1 tbsp. butter
- 4 eggs

😋 DIRECTIONS:

1. Bring the salted water to the boil and briefly cook the crabs.
2. Pass the cooking water through a hair sieve and bring to the boil in a saucepan.
3. Stir in butter and flour and let simmer. Then remove from the stove and stir until it cools down.
4. Gradually mix in the eggs and add the crabs. Let the dough rest for 15 minutes.
5. Heat oil in a pan. Bake small donuts from the batter in it.
6. Sprinkle with parsley before serving.

CIABATTA WITH FRIED TOMATOES

🦀 INGREDIENTS FOR 4 SERVINGS:

- some sugar
- ¼ kg of tomatoes
- 1 loaf of ciabatta
- 2 cloves of garlic
- some olive oil
- 1 pinch of salt and pepper
- 1 handful of basil
- 1 pinch of paprika powder
- 1-2 packs of moz.zarella

😋 DIRECTIONS:

1. Dice the tomatoes. Chop the garlic and basil. Cut the ciabatta into slices. Fry the garlic and tomatoes in a pan with olive oil. Season with basil, salt and pepper and let it steep for 5 minutes.
2. Cut the moz.zarella into small pieces.
3. Spread the fried tomatoes the ciabatta slices and cover with moz.zarella.
4. At the end sprinkle some basil over it.

CREAM CHEESE BREAD WITH VEGETABLES

 INGREDIENTS FOR 1 SERVING:

- 2 slices of whole grain rye bread
- 60 g cucumber
- salt and pepper
- ½ tsp. dill
- 50 g of grainy cream cheese
- ½ tsp. parsley
- 1 tbsp. corn kernels
- ½ tsp. chives
- 50 g cherry tomatoes
- ¼ yellow pepper

DIRECTIONS:

1. Firstly, wash and grate the cucumber. Wash and chop the herbs. Core, wash and cut the peppers into strips. Wash and quarter the tomatoes.
2. Mix the cream cheese with the herbs, cucumber and corn.
3. Then season with salt and pepper. Spread the cream cheese on the bread slices and spread the tomatoes and peppers on top.

RASPBERRIES - GRANOLA

 INGREDIENTS FOR 1 SERVING:

- 1 tsp. freshly squeezed lemon juice
- 125 g raspberries (froz.en)
- 2 tbsp. oat flakes (hearty)
- 250 g curd milk (1.5% fat)
- 5 ml of liquid sweetener

DIRECTIONS:

1. The froz.en raspberries are thawed. In the meantime, the oatmeal is mixed with the curdled milk and lemon juice.
2. The whole thing is seasoned with the sweetener. Finally, the raspberries are added and the dish can be served.

VEGETABLE FRITTATA

 INGREDIENTS FOR 8 SERVINGS:

- 1 small red bell pepper, cored, chopped
- ½ tsp. salt
- 1 small zucchini, ends trimmed, small diced
- ¼ tsp. ground black pepper
- 2 green onions, chopped
- ¼ tsp. baking powder
- 4 ounces broccoli, cut into small florets

- ⅓ cup feta cheese, crumbled
- 7 eggs
- ⅓ cup chopped parsley
- 3 tbsp. olive oil and more as needed
- 1 tsp. thyme
- ¼ cup almond milk, unsweetened

DIRECTIONS:

1. Switch on the oven, place a rimmed baking sheet in it, then set the temperature to 450 degrees F and let it preheat.
2. Take a large bowl, place broccoli, bell pepper, zucchini, onion, salt, black pepper, and oil, and then stir until well coated.
3. Remove the hot rimmed baking sheet from the oven, spread the vegetable mixture on it in an even layer, return the baking sheet into the oven and cook for 15 minutes.
4. Meanwhile, take another bowl, crack eggs in it, add baking powder, thyme, feta cheese, parsley, some salt, and black pepper, pour in the milk and then whisk until combined.
5. After 15 minutes, transfer vegetables to the egg bowland then switch heat to 400 degrees F.
6. Take an oven-proof skillet pan, coat it with oil, place the pan over medium heat and when hot, pour the egg-vegetable mixture in it and then cook for 3 minutes until eggs begin to settle.
7. Then transfer the pan into the oven and bake for 10 minutes until firm and top turn golden.
8. Meal Prep: Let the frittata cool completely, cut it into eight slices, and then wrap each slice in plastic wrap and foil. Store each frittata slice in the refrigerator for up to 5 days or freeze for up to 1 month.
9. When ready to eat, thaw afrittata slice overnight in the refrigerator, microwave for 2 to 3 minutes until hot, and then serve.

EGGPLANT SPREAD

 INGREDIENTS FOR 4 SERVINGS:

- salt and pepper
- 600 g eggplant
- 1 tsp. oregano

- 4 cloves of garlic
- 1 tbsp. lemon juice
- 250 g sheep cheese

 DIRECTIONS:

1. Preheat the oven to 180 °C.
2. Wash the eggplant, cut in half and place on a baking sheet with the cut surface facing down. Cook in the oven for 30 minutes. Then remove the stems from the eggplants.
3. Chop the garlic and cut the feta cheese in half. Puree both with the eggplants.
4. Season the spread with oregano, salt, pepper and lemon juice and cool for 30 minutes.

FRIED HAM EGGS

 INGREDIENTS FOR 4 SERVINGS:

- 4 eggs
- 2 tbsp. olive oil

- pepper
- 4 slices of Parma ham

 DIRECTIONS:

1. Boil the eggs until waxy, peel them and cut them in half lengthways. Season the cut surface.
2. Wash the sage and shake dry.
3. Halve the ham lengthways and wrap a strip around each half of the egg. Heat oil in a pan and fry the eggs on all sides.

RYE PANCAKES WITH GREEN ONION SAUCE AND RED CAVIAR

INGREDIENTS FOR 4 SERVINGS:

- 1 lb. Milk
- 3 Egg
- 4 oz. Rye flour
- 4 oz. Wheat flour
- 4 tbsp. Sour cream
- 2 oz. Red caviar
- 2 oz. Green onion

- ¼ Lemon
- tbsp. Cilantro
- 1 tbsp. Olive oil
- 1 tsp. Dijon mustard
- ½ tsp. Dry yeast
- Salt and black pepper, to taste

DIRECTIONS:

1. Beat eggs with milk, two tbsp. of sour cream, a pinch of sugar, and salt. Dissolve the yeast in a tbsp. of warm water and pour the solution into a bowl with an egg-milk mixture. Add sifted rye and wheat flour to the mixture and whisk, mix the contents of the bowl until a homogeneous liquid mass, and leave to stand for 20 minutes.
2. Blend 4 oz. of sour cream with coarsely chopped green onions, cilantro, sunflower oil, lemon quarter juice and Dijon mustard (it should be a soft greenish sauce). Mix the resulting mass with red caviar.
3. Smear the hot pan with olive oil and bake the pancakes, pouring the dough with a ladle. Do not forget to constantly lubricate the pan with oil.
4. Brush with the sauce ready pancakes, roll them in an envelope or tube. Serve hot on the table.

FRESH FRUIT AND PLAIN YOGURT

INGREDIENTS FOR 6 SERVINGS:

- ¼ fresh cantaloupe
- ¼ fresh honeydew melon
- 2 fresh kiwi
- 1 fresh peach

- 1 fresh plum
- ½ pint fresh raspberries
- 6 cups plain nonfat yogurt
- 6 mint sprigs (tops only)

DIRECTIONS:

1. Slice the cantaloupe and honeydew paper-thin (use a vegetable peeler if necessary and if the fruit is not overly ripe). Slice the kiwi into ¼-inch-thick circles. Slice the peach and plum into thin wedges. Carefully rinse the raspberries.
2. Spoon the yogurt into serving bowls and arrange the fruits decoratively around each rim. (The cantaloupe and melon can be arranged like a lacy border; the other cut fruit can be fanned and placed atop the yogurt.) Sprinkle the raspberries on top. Garnish with mint.

FRIED CHEESE TOAST

INGREDIENTS FOR 4 SERVINGS:

- 200 ml of milk
- 2 eggs
- 4 slices of ham
- 1 pinch of paprika powder

- 4 slices of Emmentaler
- 1 pinch of chili pepper
- Oil / 8 slices of toast

DIRECTIONS:

1. Cover 4 slices of toast with ham and cheese and cover with the other slices of toast.
2. Mix the eggs, paprika, milk, nutmeg and chili together.
3. Heat oil in a pan.
4. Turn the sandwiches in the egg mixture and fry on both sides in the pan. As soon as the cheese has melted, serve the toast.

FRITTATA

 INGREDIENTS FOR 6 SERVINGS:

- 1 pound Idaho potatoes
- 2 each yellow and red peppers
- 2 Italian green peppers
- 1 large red onion
- ½ cup fresh oregano
- 3 ounces fontina cheese
- 2 tsp. olive oil

- Kosher or sea salt, to taste
- Fresh-cracked black pepper, to taste
- 3 whole eggs
- 6 egg whites
- 1 cup plain nonfat yogurt
- 1 cup skim milk

 DIRECTIONS:

1. Preheat oven to 375°F.
2. Slice the potatoes into large pieces. Stem, seed, and slice the peppers. Cut the onion into thick slices. Chop the oregano leaves. Grate the fontina.
3. Separately toss the potatoes, peppers, and onion in oil, and drain on a rack. Season with salt and black pepper.
4. Roast all the vegetables separately in the oven until partially cooked. Layer all in a baking dish.
5. Whisk together the eggs, egg whites, yogurt, milk, and grated cheese; pour into the baking dish.
6. Bake until the egg mixture is completely set, approximately 30 to 45 minutes. Sprinkle with chopped oregano and serve.

RICOTTA FIG OATMEAL

 INGREDIENTS FOR 1 SERVINGS:

- ½ cup Old fashioned rolled oats
- 2 tbsp. Dried figs (chopped)
- 1 cup Water
- 2 tbsp. Ricotta cheese (part-skim)

- 2 tsp. Honey
- Salt (Just a pinch)
- 1 tbsp. Toasted almonds (sliced)

 DIRECTIONS:

1. Place the water and salt in a pan and bring to boil.
2. Mix in the oats and reduce the flame, stir cooking for 5
3. Minute still almost all liquid is absorbed.
4. Top with the remaining ingredients.

FRIED EGG IN A BED OF VEGETABLES

 INGREDIENTS FOR 4 SERVINGS:

- butter
- Paprika powder / parsley
- salt and pepper
- 2 green mild chili peppers

- 4 eggs / 2 peppers
- 50 g feta
- 1 spring onion / 4 tomatoes

DIRECTIONS:

1. Dice the spring onions. Core the peppers and chili and cut into strips.
2. Pour hot water over the tomatoes, peel them and cut into small pieces.
3. Heat the butter in a pan. Steam the spring onions with the chili and paprika. Then add the tomatoes.
4. Chop the parsley and add to the vegetables along with salt and pepper.
5. Make 4 hollows in the vegetable mixture. Beat an egg in each well. Season this with salt and sprinkle with feta cheese.
6. Arrange the finished fried egg in portions in the bed of vegetables.

ALMOND MASCARPONE DUMPLINGS

 INGREDIENTS FOR 4 SERVINGS:

- 1 cup whole-wheat flour
- 1 cup all-purpose unbleached flour
- ¼ cup ground almonds4 egg whites
- 3 ounces mascarpone cheese

- 1 tsp. extra-virgin olive oil
- 2 tsp. apple juice
- 1 tbsp. butter
- ¼ cup honey

DIRECTIONS:

1. Sift together both types of flour in a large bowl. Mix in the almonds. In a separate bowl, cream together the egg whites, cheese, oil, and juice on medium speed with an electric mixer.
2. Combine the flour and egg white mixture with a dough hook on medium speed or by hand until a dough forms.
3. Boil 1 gallon water in a medium-size saucepot. Take a spoonful of the dough and use a second spoon to push it into the boiling water. Cook until the dumpling floats to the top, about 5 to 10 minutes. You can cook several dumplings at once;just take care not to crowd the pot. Remove with a slotted spoon and drain on paper towels.
4. Heat a medium-size sauté pan on medium-high heat. Add the butter, then place the dumplings in the pan and cook until light brown.
5. Place on serving plates and drizzle with honey.

CIABATTA ROLLS WITH AVOCADO

 INGREDIENTS FOR 4 SERVINGS:

- salt and pepper
- olive oil
- Lemon juice
- Iceberg lettuce
- 2-3 tomatoes

- 2 ciabatta rolls
- 2 avocados
- 16 slices of Par ma ham
- 4 hard-boiled eggs

DIRECTIONS:

1. Peel and slice the eggs. Core the avocado, cut the flesh into strips and drizzle with lemon juice. Cut the tomatoes into slices. Halve the rolls and toast the inside without fat. Then drizzle with oil and season with pepper.
2. Cover the bottom of the rolls with the ham. Place the eggs, avocado and tomatoes on top. Spread the rest of the ham on top and place the other half of the bun on top. Serve the sandwiches with salad.

SIMPLE OMELETTE

 INGREDIENTS FOR 4 SERVINGS:

- 2 tbsp. parmesan
- 12 eggs
- salt and pepper
- 12 tbsp. chopped herbs

- ⅛ l milk
- 6 tbsp. butter
- 1 tbsp. flour

DIRECTIONS:

1. Work the eggs with flour, milk, parmesan, salt and pepper into dough. Melt the butter in a pan and steam the herbs in it.
2. Pour the batter over the herbs in the pan and stir.
3. Fry the omelette on both sides and serve.

VEGETABLE STICKS WITH DIP

 INGREDIENTS FOR 2 SERVINGS:

- 1 clove of garlic
- 1 egg yolk
- salt and pepper
- 2 tbsp. of pickle water
- 4 basil leaves
- 2 tsp. of balsamic vinegar

- 80 ml of olive oil
- 1 pinch of Dijon mustard
- 100 g canned shredded tuna
- Vegetables of your choice
- 1 tbsp. chopped capers

 DIRECTIONS:

1. Wash, peel and cut the vegetables of your choice into sticks.
2. Puree the egg yolk with the capers, tuna, pickle water, mustard, basil, olive oil, balsamic vinegar and garlic.
3. Pass the dip through a sieve and season with salt and pepper. Serve the dip with the vegetable sticks.

EGGS WITH TRUFFLE OIL

 INGREDIENTS FOR 2 SERVINGS:

- 1 tbsp. truffle oil
- 100 g peeled and cooked shrimp
- white pepper from the mill
- 3 egg yolks

- Sea salt from the mill
- 125 ml of milk
- 125 ml low-fat whipped cream

 DIRECTIONS:

1. Heat the water in a saucepan and whip the milk, whipped cream, truffle oil and egg yolks in a steam bath while stirring constantly. The egg should start to thaw.
2. The shrimp are roughly chopped and carefully lifted into the truffle-egg mixture. Finally, everything is seasoned with the salt and pepper.

BREAKFAST GRANOLA

 INGREDIENTS FOR 6 SERVING:

- ½ cup oats
- 1 tsp. ground cinnamon
- ⅓ cup sliced almonds
- 2 tbsp. shredded coconut

- 2 tbsp. sunflower seeds
- 1 tbsp. flax seeds
- 1 tsp. coconut oil
- 2 tbsp. honey

DIRECTIONS:

1. Take a medium bowl, place all the ingredients in it and then stir until well mixed.
2. Take a skillet pan, place it over medium heat, add the granola mixture and then cook for 3 to 5 minutes until toasted.
3. Meal Prep: Let the granola cool completely, place it in an air-tight jar and then seal it.
4. When ready to eat, one-sixth place portion of the granola in a bowl, add milk, top with fruit slices,
5. And then serve.

CHAPTER 3: SEAFOOD/FISH

BROILED BLUEFISH WITH PRESERVED LEMON AND ZHOUG

🐟 INGREDIENTS FOR 4 SERVINGS:

- 4 (4 to 6-ounce) skinless blueish illets, 1 to 1½ inches thick
- Salt and pepper
- ¼ cup mayonnaise
- ¼ preserved lemon, pulp and white pith removed, rind rinsed and minced (1 tbsp.)
- 1 garlic clove, minced
- ¼ tsp. sugar
- ¼ cup Green Zhoug
- Lemon wedges

⚙ DIRECTIONS:

1. Adjust oven rack 4 inches from broiler element and heat broiler. Pat bluefish dry with paper towels, season with salt and pepper, and place skinned side down in greased rimmed baking sheet.
2. Combine mayonnaise, preserved lemon, garlic, and sugar in bowl, then spread mixture evenly on tops of fillets. Broil until bluefish flakes apart when gently prodded with paring knife and registers 140 degrees, about 5 minutes. Serve with Green Zhoug and lemon wedges.

BRAISED HALIBUT WITH LEEKS AND MUSTARD

INGREDIENTS FOR 4 SERVINGS:

- 4 (4- to 6-ounce) skinless halibut illets, ¾ to 1 inch thick
- Salt and pepper
- ¼ cup extra-virgin olive oil, plus extra for serving
- 1 pound leeks, white and light green parts only, halved lengthwise, sliced thin, and washed thoroughly
- 1 tsp. Dijon mustard
- ¾ cup dry white wine
- 1 tbsp. minced fresh parsley
- Lemon wedges

DIRECTIONS:

1. Pat halibut dry with paper towels and sprinkle with ½ tsp. salt. Heat oil in 12-inch skillet over medium heat until warm, about 15 seconds. Place halibut skinned side up in skillet and cook until bottom half of halibut begins to turn opaque (halibut should not brown), about 4 minutes. Carefully transfer halibut raw side down to large plate.
2. Add leeks, mustard, and ¼ tsp. salt to oil left in skillet and cook over medium heat, stirring frequently, until softened, 10 to 12 minutes. Stir in wine and bring to simmer. Place halibut raw side down on top of leeks. Reduce heat to medium-low, cover, and simmer gently until halibut flakes apart when gently prodded with paring knife and registers 140 degrees, 6 to 10 minutes. Carefully transfer halibut to serving platter, tent loosely with aluminum foil, and let rest while finishing leeks.
3. Return leeks to high heat and simmer briskly until mixture is thickened slightly, 2 to 4 minutes. Season with salt and pepper to taste. Arrange leek mixture around halibut, drizzle with extra oil, and sprinkle with parsley. Serve with lemon wedges.

PAN-ROASTED SEA BASS WITH WILD MUSHROOMS

 INGREDIENTS FOR 4 SERVINGS:

- ½ cup water
- ⅓ ounce dried porcini mushrooms
- 4 (4 to 6-ounce) skinless sea bass illets, 1 to 1½ inches thick ¼ cup extra virgin olive oil, plus extra for serving
- Salt and pepper
- 1 sprig fresh rosemary
- 1 red onion, halved and sliced thin
- 12 ounces portobello mushroom caps, halved and sliced ½ inch thick
- 1 pound cremini mushrooms, trimmed and halved if small or quartered if large
- 2 garlic cloves, minced
- 1 tbsp. minced fresh parsley
- Lemon wedges

 DIRECTIONS:

1. Microwave water and porcini mushrooms in covered bowl until steaming, about 1 minute. Let sit until softened, about 5 minutes. Drain mushrooms in fine-mesh strainer lined with cofee filter, reserve porcini liquid, and mince mushrooms.
2. Adjust oven rack to lower-middle position and heat oven to 475 degrees. Pat sea bass dry with paper towels, rub with 2 tbsp. oil, and season with salt and pepper.
3. Heat remaining 2 tbsp. oil and rosemary in 12-inch ovensafe skillet over medium-high heat until shimmering. Add onion, portobello mushrooms, cremini mushrooms, and ½ tsp. salt. Cook, stirring occasionally, until mushrooms have released their liquid and are beginning to brown, 8 to 10 minutes. Stir in garlic and porcini mushrooms and cook until fragrant, about 30 seconds.
4. Of heat, stir in reserved porcini liquid. Nestle sea bass skinned side down into skillet, transfer to oven, and roast until fish flakes apart when gently prodded with paring knife and registers 140 degrees, 10 to 12 minutes. Sprinkle with parsley and drizzle with extra oil. Serve with lemon wedges.

SICILIAN FISH STEW

 INGREDIENTS FOR 4 SERVINGS:

- ¼ cup pine nuts, toasted
- ¼ cup chopped fresh mint
- 4 garlic cloves, minced
- 1 tsp. grated orange zest
- 2 tbsp. extra-virgin olive oil
- 2 onions, chopped ine
- 1 celery rib, minced
- Salt and pepper
- 1 tsp. minced fresh thyme or ¼ tsp. dried
- Pinch red pepper lakes
- ½ cup dry white wine
- 1 (28-ounce) can whole peeled tomatoes, drained with juice reserved, chopped coarse
- 2 (8-ounce) bottles clam juice
- ¼ cup golden raisins
- 2 tbsp. capers, rinsed
- 1½ pounds skinless swordish steaks, 1 to 1 ½ inches thick, cut into 1-inch pieces

 DIRECTIONS:

1. Combine pine nuts, mint, one-quarter of garlic, and orange zest in bowl; set aside for serving. Heat oil in Dutch oven over medium heat until shimmering. Add onions, celery, ½ tsp. salt, and ¼ tsp. pepper and cook until softened, about 5 minutes. Stir in thyme, pepper flakes, and remaining garlic and cook until fragrant, about 30 seconds.
2. Stir in wine and reserved tomato juice, bring to simmer, and cook until reduced by half, about 4 minutes. Stir in tomatoes, clam juice, raisins, and capers,bring to simmer, and cook until flavors meld, about 15 minutes.
3. Pat swordfish dry with paper towels and season with salt and pepper. Nestle swordfish into pot and spoon some cooking liquid over top. Bring to simmer and cook for 4 minutes. Of heat, cover and let sit until swordfish flakes apart when gently prodded with paring knife, about 3 minutes. Season with salt and pepper to taste. Serve, sprinkling individual bowls with pine nut mixture.

SEARED SCALLOPS WITH ORANGE-LIME DRESSING

INGREDIENTS FOR 4 SERVINGS:

- 1½ pounds large sea scallops, tendons removed
- 6 tbsp. extra-virgin olive oil
- 2 tbsp. orange juice
- 2 tbsp. lime juice
- 1 small shallot, minced
- 1 tbsp. minced fresh cilantro
- ⅛ tsp. red pepper lakes
- Salt and pepper

DIRECTIONS:

1. Place scallops in rimmed baking sheet lined with clean kitchen towel. Place second clean kitchen towel on top of scallops and press gently on towel to blot liquid. Let scallops sit at room temperature, covered with towel, for 10 minutes.
2. Whisk ¼ cup oil, orange juice, lime juice, shallot, cilantro, and pepper flakes together in bowl. Season with salt to taste and set aside for serving.
3. Heat 1 tbsp. oil in 12-inch nonstick skillet over medium-high heat until just smoking. Add half of scallops to skillet in single layer and cook, without moving them, until well browned on first side, about 1½ minutes. Flip scallops and continue to cook, without moving them, until well browned on second side, about 1½ minutes. Transfer scallops to serving platter and tent loosely with aluminum foil. Repeat with remaining 1 tbsp. oil and remaining scallops. Whisk dressing to recombine and serve with scallops.

CALAMARI STEW WITH GARLIC AND TOMATOES

INGREDIENTS FOR 4 SERVINGS:

- ¼ cup extra-virgin olive oil, plus extra for serving
- 2 onions, chopped ine
- 2 celery ribs, sliced thin
- 8 garlic cloves, minced
- ¼ tsp. red pepper lakes
- ½ cup dry white wine or dry vermouth
- 2 pounds small squid, bodies sliced crosswise into 1-inch-thick rings, tentacles halved
- Salt and pepper
- 3 (28-ounce) cans whole peeled tomatoes, drained and chopped coarse ⅓ cup pitted brine-cured green olives, chopped coarse
- 1 tbsp. capers, rinsed
- 3 tbsp. minced fresh parsley

DIRECTIONS:

1. Heat oil in Dutch oven over medium-high heat until shimmering. Add onions and celery and cook until softened, about 5 minutes. Stir in garlic and pepper flakes and cook until fragrant, about 30 seconds. Stir in wine, scraping up any browned bits, and cook until nearly evaporated, about 1 minute.
2. Pat squid dry with paper towels and season with salt and pepper. Stir squid into pot. Reduce heat to medium-low, cover, and simmer gently until squid has released its liquid, about 15 minutes. Stir in tomatoes, olives, and capers, cover, and continue to cook until squid is very tender, 30 to 35 minutes.
3. Of heat, stir in parsley and season with salt and pepper to taste. Serve, drizzling individual portions with extra oil.

SWORDFISH EN COCOTTE WITH SHALLOTS, CUCUMBER, AND MINT

 INGREDIENTS FOR 4 SERVINGS:

- ¾ cup fresh mint leaves
- ¼ cup fresh parsley leaves
- 5 tbsp. extra-virgin olive oil
- 2 tbsp. lemon juice
- 4 garlic cloves, minced
- 1 tsp. ground cumin

- ¼ tsp. cayenne pepper
- Salt and pepper
- 3 shallots, sliced thin
- 1 cucumber, peeled, seeded, and sliced thin
- 4 (4 to 6-ounce) skin-on swordish steaks, 1 to 1½ inches thick

DIRECTIONS:

1. Adjust oven rack to lowest position and heat oven to 250 degrees. Process mint, parsley, 3 tbsp. oil, lemon juice, garlic, cumin, cayenne, and ¼ tsp. salt in food processor until smooth, about 20 seconds, scraping down sides of bowl as needed.
2. Heat remaining 2 tbsp. oil in Dutch oven over medium-low heat until shimmering. Add shallots, cover, and cook, stirring occasionally, until softened, about 5 minutes. Of heat, stir in processed mint mixture and cucumber.
3. Pat swordfish dry with paper towels and season with salt and pepper. Place swordfish on top of cucumber-mint mixture. Place large sheet of aluminum foil over pot and press to seal, then cover tightly with lid. Transfer pot to oven and cook until swordfish flakes apart when gently prodded with paring knife and registers 140 degrees, 35 to 40 minutes.
4. Carefully transfer swordfish to serving platter. Season cucumber- mint mixture with salt and pepper to taste, then spoon over swordfish.

HEALTHY TUNA & BEAN WRAPS

 INGREDIENTS FOR 4 SERVINGS:

- 15 oz. canned cannellini beans, drained and rinsed
- 12 oz. canned light tuna in water, drained and flaked
- ⅛ tsp. white pepper
- ⅛ tsp. kosher salt
- 1 tbsp. fresh parsley, chopped

- 2 tbsp. extra-virgin avocado oil
- ¼ cup red onion, chopped
- 12 romaine lettuce leaves
- 1 medium-sized ripe Hass avocado, sliced

DIRECTIONS:

1. In a large mixing bowl, stir together the beans, tuna, pepper, salt, parsley, avocado oil, and red onions.
2. Spoon some of the mixture onto each lettuce leaf, and top with the sliced avocado before folding and serving.

OLIVE BAKED COD FILLETS

INGREDIENTS FOR 4 SERVINGS:

- 4 cod fillets
- 2 tbsp. extra-virgin avocado oil
- ¼ tsp. kosher salt
- ⅛ tsp. white pepper
- ½ small shallot, thinly sliced

- 1 small green pepper, thinly sliced
- ¼ cup Kalamata olives, pitted and chopped
- 8 oz. canned tomato sauce
- ¼ cup moz.zarella cheese, grated

DIRECTIONS:

1. Set the oven to preheat to 400°F, with the wire rack in the center of the oven. Coat a large casserole dish with baking spray.
2. Arrange the cod fillets in the prepared casserole dish. Use a basting brush to coat the fillets with the oil, and season with the salt and pepper. Top the seasoned fillets with the shallots, green peppers, and olives. Pour the tomato sauce over everything in the dish, and top with the cheese.
3. Bake in the oven for 15-20 minutes, or until the fish is flaky and opaque.

GREEK-STYLE PAN-ROASTED SWORDFISH

 INGREDIENTS FOR 4 SERVINGS:

- 4 tbsp. extra-virgin avocado oil (divided)
- 1 small shallot, thinly sliced
- 2 tsp. crushed garlic
- ½ medium eggplant, diced
- 2 medium zucchinis, diced
- 1 cup whole Greek olives, pitted

- 2 cups cherry tomatoes, halved
- 4 skin-on swordfish fillets, patted dry
- Himalayan salt
- Freshly ground black pepper
- ¼ cup green olive tapenade with harissa

 DIRECTIONS:

1. Set the oven to preheat to 375°F, with the wire rack in the center of the oven.
2. Heat 2 tbsp. of oil in a large frying pan over medium-high heat. When the oil is nice and hot, fry the shallots and garlic for about 5 minutes, or until the shallots become translucent. Stir in the eggplant, and fry until it starts to become tender – about 3 minutes. Add the zucchini, and stir for an additional 5 minutes, until all of the vegetables are fork-tender, and crispy around the edges. Stir in the olives and tomatoes, and fry, and stirring for 2 minutes. Set the pan aside, off the heat.
3. Season the fish generously with salt and pepper. Heat the remaining olive oil in an oven-proof pan over medium-high heat. When the oil is nice and hot, place the fish fillets skin down in the pan, and fry for 3 minutes. The edges should just begin to become solid. Flip the fish in the pan before transferring to the oven, and baking for a final 3 minutes. The fish should be completely solid and flaky when done.
4. Top the cooked swordfish with fried vegetables and olive tapenade. Serve immediately.

OLIVE OIL LEMON BROILED COD

 INGREDIENTS FOR 4 SERVINGS:

- 4 cod fillets
- 1 tsp. dried marjoram
- 4 tbsp. olive oil

- 1 lemon, juiced
- 1 thyme sprig
- Salt and pepper to taste

 DIRECTIONS:

1. Season the cod with salt, pepper and marjoram.
2. Heat the oil in a large skillet and place the cod in the hot oil.
3. Fry on medium heat on both sides until golden brown then add the lemon juice.
4. Place the thyme sprig on top and cover with a lid.
5. Cook for 5 more minutes then remove from heat.
6. Serve the cod and sauce fresh.

SPICY CRUSTED SALMON

 INGREDIENTS FOR 4 SERVINGS:

- 4 salmon fillets
- 1 tsp. chili powder
- 1 tsp. mustard powder

- 1 tsp. cumin powder
- Salt and pepper to taste
- ½ cup ground almonds

DIRECTIONS:

1. Mix the ground almonds, chili powder, mustard powder and cumin in a bowl.
2. Season the salmon with salt and pepper.
3. Roll each fillet of fish into the almond mixture then place them in a baking tray.
4. Bake in the preheated oven at 350F for 15 minutes.
5. Serve the salmon fresh and warm.

CHORIZO FISH STEW

 INGREDIENTS FOR 6 SERVINGS:

- 2 tbsp. olive oil
- 2 shallots, chopped
- 2 garlic cloves, minced
- 1 celery stalk, chopped
- 2 carrots, diced
- 2 leeks, sliced
- 2 chorizo links, sliced

- 1 cup diced tomatoes
- ¼ cup white wine
- 2 potatoes, peeled and cubed
- 2 cups vegetable stock
- 6 cod fillets
- Salt and pepper to taste
- 2 tbsp. lemon juice

DIRECTIONS:

1. Heat the oil in a saucepan and stir in the shallots and garlic, celery and carrots, as well as carrots.
2. Cook for 5 minutes then add the chorizo and cook for another 5 minutes.
3. Add the rest of the ingredients, except the fish and lemon juice and season with salt and pepper.
4. Cook on low heat for 20 minutes then add the cod and lemon juice and continue cooking for 5 more minutes.
5. Serve the stew warm and fresh.

GRILLED PESTO SALMON

 INGREDIENTS FOR 4 SERVINGS:

- 4 salmon fillets
- 4 tbsp. pesto sauce

- Salt and pepper to taste

DIRECTIONS:

1. Season the salmon with salt and pepper and spread the pesto over the fish.
2. Heat a grill pan over medium flame and place the salmon on the grill.
3. Cook on each side for 5 minutes.
4. Serve the salmon fresh and warm.

GRILLED SALMON WITH BUTTERNUT SQUASH PUREE

 INGREDIENTS FOR 6 SERVINGS:

- 6 salmon fillets
- 3 tbsp. olive oil
- 1 butternut squash, peeled and cubed

- 1 tsp. smoked paprika
- Salt and pepper to taste
- 2 tbsp. butter

 DIRECTIONS:

1. Season the salmon with salt and pepper and drizzle with olive oil.
2. Heat a grill pan over medium flame and place the salmon on the grill.
3. Cook on each side for 5 minutes.
4. In the meantime, season the squash with salt, pepper and paprika and cook it in a steamer.
5. When the butternut is soft, puree it in a blender with the puree.
6. Serve the salmon with the puree.

ASPARAGUS BAKED PLAICE

INGREDIENTS FOR 4 SERVINGS:

- 4 plaice fillets
- 2 cups cherry tomatoes
- 1 bunch asparagus, trimmed and halved
- ½ lemon, juiced
- 2 tbsp. olive oil
- Salt and pepper to taste

DIRECTIONS:

1. Combine the tomatoes, asparagus, lemon juice and oil in a deep dish baking pan. Season with salt and pepper.
2. Place the fillets on top and cook in the preheated oven at 350F for 15 minutes.
3. Serve the plaice and the veggies warm and fresh.

LEMON-HERB HAKE FILLETS WITH GARLIC POTATOES

INGREDIENTS FOR 4 SERVINGS:

- 1½ pounds russet potatoes, unpeeled, sliced into ¼-inch-thick rounds
- ¼ cup extra-virgin olive oil
- 3 garlic cloves, minced
- Salt and pepper
- 4 (4 to 6-ounce) skinless hake illets, 1 to 1½ inches thick
- 4 sprigs fresh thyme
- 1 lemon, sliced thin

DIRECTIONS:

1. Adjust oven rack to lower-middle position and heat oven to 425 degrees. Toss potatoes with 2 tbsp. oil and garlic in bowl and season with salt and pepper. Microwave, uncovered, until potatoes are just tender, 12 to 14 minutes, stirring halfway through microwaving.
2. Transfer potatoes to 13 by 9-inch baking dish and press gently into even layer. Pat hake dry with paper towels, season with salt and pepper, and arrange skinned side down on top of potatoes. Drizzle hake with remaining 2 tbsp. oil, then place thyme sprigs and lemon slices on top. Bake until hake flakes apart when gently prodded with paring knife and registers 140 degrees, 15 to 18 minutes. Slide spatula underneath potatoes and hake and carefully transfer to individual plates.

GRILLED SWORDFISH WITH ITALIAN SALSA VERDE

INGREDIENTS FOR 4 SERVINGS:

- 4 (4 to 6-ounce) skin-on swordfish steaks, 1 to 1½ inches thick 2 tbsp. extra-virgin olive oil
- Salt and pepper
- ½ cup Italian Salsa Verde

DIRECTIONS:

1. Pat swordfish dry with paper towels, rub with oil, and season with salt and pepper.
2. 2a. FOR A CHARCOAL GRILL Open bottom vent completely. Light large chimney starter filled with charcoal briquettes (6 quarts). When top coals are partially covered with ash, pour two-thirds evenly over half of grill, then pour remaining coals over other half of grill. Set cooking grate in place, cover, and open lid vent completely. Heat grill until hot, about 5 minutes.
3. 2b. FOR A GAS GRILL Turn all burners to high, cover, and heat grill until hot, about 15 minutes. Leave primary burner on high and turn other burner(s) to medium-high.
4. Clean cooking grate, then repeatedly brush grate with well-oiled paper towels until black and glossy, 5 to 10 times. Place swordfish on hotter part of grill and cook, uncovered, until streaked with dark grill marks, 6 to 9 minutes, gently flipping steaks using 2 spatulas halfway through cooking.
5. Gently move swordfish to cooler part of grill and continue to cook, uncovered, until fish flakes apart when gently prodded with paring knife and registers 140 degrees, 1 to 3 minutes per side. Serve with Italian Salsa Verde.

VEGETABLE BRAISED BLACK SEA BASS

 INGREDIENTS FOR 6 SERVINGS:

- 6 black sea bass fillets
- 2 sweet onions, sliced
- 6 garlic cloves, chopped
- 2 cups cherry tomatoes
- ¼ cup dry white wine
- ½ cup vegetable stock
- 1 bay leaf
- 1 thyme sprig
- Salt and pepper to taste

DIRECTIONS:

1. Combine the onions, garlic, tomatoes, wine, stock, bay leaf and thyme in a deep dish baking pan.
2. Place the fish over the veggies and season with salt and pepper.
3. Cover the pan with aluminum foil and cook in the preheated oven at 350F for 30 minutes.
4. Serve the sea bass and vegetables fresh.

SPICED SEARED SCALLOPS WITH LEMON RELISH

 INGREDIENTS FOR 4 SERVINGS:

- 2 pounds scallops, cleaned
- ½ tsp. cumin powder
- ¼ tsp. ground ginger
- ½ tsp. ground coriander
- ½ tsp. smoked paprika
- ½ tsp. salt
- 3 tbsp. olive oil

DIRECTIONS:

1. Pat the scallops dry with a paper towel.
2. Sprinkle them with spices and salt.
3. Heat the oil in a skillet and place half of the scallops in the hot oil. Cook for 1-2 minutes per side, just until the scallops look golden brown on the sides.
4. Remove the scallops and place the remaining ones in the hot oil.
5. Serve the scallops warm and fresh with your favorite side dish.

MIXED VEGGIE FISH TAGINE

 INGREDIENTS FOR 6 SERVINGS:

- 6 cod fillets
- 3 tbsp. olive oil
- 4 garlic cloves, chopped
- 2 red bell peppers, cored and sliced
- 2 yellow bell peppers, cored and sliced
- 1 carrot, sliced
- 1 celery stalk, sliced
- 1 jalapeno, sliced
- 2 tomatoes, sliced
- 1 tsp. cumin powder
- 1 zucchini, sliced
- ¼ cup dry white wine
- ¼ cup green olives
- ½ lemon, juiced
- Salt and pepper to taste

DIRECTIONS:

1. Combine the oil, garlic, peppers, carrot, celery, jalapeno, tomatoes, cumin, zucchini and wine in a deep dish baking pan.
2. Place the cod on top and season with salt and pepper.
3. Sprinkle with olives and drizzle with lemon juice.
4. Cover the pan with aluminum foil and cook in the preheated oven at 350F for 30 minutes.
5. Serve the dish warm and fresh.

CHAPTER 4: MEAT/POULTRY

PAN-SEARED CHICKEN BREASTS WITH CHICKPEA SALAD

 INGREDIENTS FOR 4 SERVINGS:

- 6 tbsp. extra-virgin olive oil
- ¼ cup lemon juice (2 lemons)
- 1 tsp. honey
- 1 tsp. smoked paprika
- ½ tsp. ground cumin
- Salt and pepper
- 2 (15-ounce) cans chickpeas, rinsed
- ½ red onion, sliced thin
- ¼ cup chopped fresh mint
- ½ cup all-purpose lour
- 4 (4- to 6-ounce) boneless, skinless chicken breasts, trimmed

DIRECTIONS:

1. Whisk ¼ cup oil, lemon juice, honey, paprika, cumin, ½ tsp. salt, and ½ tsp. pepper together in large bowl until combined. Reserve 3 tbsp. dressing for serving. Add chickpeas, onion, and mint to remaining dressing and toss to combine. Season with salt and pepper to taste and set aside for serving.
2. Spread flour in shallow dish. Pound thicker ends of chicken breasts between 2 sheets of plastic wrap to uniform ½-inch thickness. Pat chicken dry with paper towels and season with salt and pepper. Working with 1 chicken breast at a time, dredge in flour to coat, shaking of any excess.
3. Heat remaining 2 tbsp. oil in 12-inch skillet over medium-high heat until just smoking. Place chicken in skillet and cook, turning as needed, until golden brown on both sides and chicken registers 160 degrees, about 10 minutes. Transfer chicken to serving platter, tent loosely with aluminum foil, and let rest for 5 minutes. Drizzle reserved dressing over chicken and serve with salad.

ZESTY, LETTUCE-WRAPPED CHICKEN GYROS

 INGREDIENTS FOR 4 SERVINGS:

- 1 ½ lbs. boneless chicken breasts, skins removed
- ½ tsp. white pepper
- ½ tsp. kosher salt
- ½ tsp. dried thyme
- ½ tsp. dried oregano
- ½ tsp. ground cumin
- 1 tsp. crushed garlic
- 2 tbsp. freshly squeezed lemon juice
- 1 lemon, zested
- 8 outer leaves of romaine lettuce
- Tahini sauce
- 4 thin dill pickle spears
- Very thinly sliced red onion
- 1 heirloom tomato, sliced

 DIRECTIONS:

1. Place the chicken breasts on a wooden chopping board, and cover with greaseproof paper. Pound the breasts, using a wooden mallet, to about ¼-inches thick, before slicing into 6 strips.
2. In a large bowl, whisk together the pepper, salt, thyme, oregano, cumin, garlic, lemon juice, and lemon zest. Add the chicken strips, and toss to coat. Cover the bowl in cling wrap, and chill overnight, or for a minimum of 30 minutes.
3. When the chicken is properly chilled, preheat the oven broiler on low, with the wire rack about 6-inches away from the broiler. Arrange the chicken strips on a foil-covered baking sheet, and broil in the oven for 7 minutes, or until the chicken is just properly cooked.
4. Place the lettuce leaves on a plate, and top each leaf with a generous dollop of tahini sauce, followed by the dill spears, red onions, and tomato slices. Divide the cooked chicken between the leaves, fold, and serve.

VEGETABLE & HERB CHICKEN CACCIATORE

 INGREDIENTS FOR 6 SERVINGS:

- 1 cup boiling water
- ½ oz. dried porcini mushrooms
- 2 tbsp. avocado oil
- 12 boneless chicken thighs, skins removed and fat trimmed
- 1 large fennel bulb, cored, halved, and thinly sliced
- 1 large shallot, halved and thinly sliced
- 1 large green bell pepper, seeded, and chopped into rings
- 1 tsp. fresh thyme leaves, chopped
- 2 tsp. finely grated orange zest
- 1 tbsp. fresh rosemary, chopped
- 3 tsp. crushed garlic
- 3 tbsp. balsamic vinegar
- 1 tsp. kosher salt
- 2 tbsp. tomato paste
- ¾ cup dry white wine

 DIRECTIONS:

1. Set the oven to preheat to 350°F, with the wire rack in the center of the oven.
2. Place the boiling water and mushrooms in a large bowl, and allow to soak on the counter for 20 minutes.
3. Meanwhile, heat the olive oil in a large frying pan over medium-high heat, before adding the chicken thighs, and browning on all sides. Cook the chicken in batches if needed, to avoid overcrowding the pan. Transfer the cooked thighs to a large casserole dish.
4. Lower the heat, and add the fennel, shallots, and bell pepper to the same pan, frying for about 5 minutes, or until the vegetables are fork-tender. Add the thyme, zest, rosemary, and garlic. Fry for 30 seconds before adding the vinegar, and frying for an additional 1 minute.
5. Finely chop the soaked mushrooms before adding them to the pan, along with the soaking water, salt, tomato paste, and wine.
6. Once the sauce begins to boil, carefully pour the contents of the pan over the thighs in the casserole dish. Cover the dish with foil, and bake for 45 minutes.
7. Allow the cooked thighs to stand on the counter for 5-10 minutes before serving hot.

SPICE CRUSTED LAMB CHOPS

 INGREDIENTS FOR 6 SERVINGS:

- 6 lamb chops
- ½ cup breadcrumbs
- ½ cup almond flour
- 1 tsp. cumin powder
- 1 tsp. ground coriander
- 1 tsp. dried sage
- 1 tsp. chili powder
- Salt and pepper to taste
- 3 tbsp. olive oil

 DIRECTIONS:

1. Mix the breadcrumbs, almond flour, spices and herbs in a bowl. Add salt and pepper as well.
2. Drizzle the lamb chops with oil and rub the meat well with the oil.
3. Roll each lamb chopinto the crumb mixture and place them all in a deep dish baking tray.
4. Cook in the preheated oven at 350F for 20 minutes.
5. Serve the lamb chops warm.

HERBED LAMB CUTLETS WITH ROASTED VEGETABLES

 INGREDIENTS FOR 10 SERVINGS:

- 10 lamb cutlets
- 2 red bell peppers, cored and sliced
- 2 sweet potatoes, peeled and cubed
- 2 zucchinis, cubed
- 2 tomatoes, sliced
- 2 carrots, sliced
- 2 parsnips, sliced
- 1 celery root, peeled and sliced
- 1 red onion, quartered
- 4 garlic cloves, crushed
- 3 tbsp. olive oil
- Salt and pepper to taste
- 2 tbsp. lemon juice
- 1 rosemary sprig
- 1 thyme sprig

DIRECTIONS:

1. Combine the vegetables, oil, salt, pepper and lemon juice in a deep dish baking pan.
2. Add salt and pepper, as well as lemon juice, rosemary and thyme.
3. Season the lamb with salt and pepper and place it over the vegetables.
4. Cook in the preheated oven at 350F for 45 minutes.
5. Serve the lamb and veggies warm and fresh.

ZA'ATAR-RUBBED BUTTERFLIED CHICKEN

 INGREDIENTS FOR 4 SERVINGS:

- 2 tbsp. za'atar
- 5 tbsp. plus 1 tsp. extra-virgin olive oil
- 1 (3½ - to 4-pound) whole chicken, giblets discarded
- Salt and pepper
- 1 tbsp. minced fresh mint
- ¼ preserved lemon, pulp and white pith removed, rind rinsed and minced (1 tbsp.)
- 2 tsp. white wine vinegar
- ½ tsp. Dijon mustard

 DIRECTIONS:

1. Adjust oven rack to lowest position and heat oven to 450 degrees. Combine za 'atar and 2 tbsp. oil in small bowl. With chicken breast side down, use kitchen shears to cut through bones on either side of backbone. Discard backbone and trim away excess fat and skin around neck. Flip chicken and tuck wingtips behind back. Press firmly on breastbone to flatten, then pound breast to be same thickness as legs and thighs. Pat chicken dry with paper towels and season with salt and pepper.
2. Heat 1 tsp. oil in 12-inch ovensafe skillet over medium-high heat until just smoking. Place chicken skin side down in skillet, reduce heat to medium, and place heavy pot on chicken to press it flat. Cook chicken until skin is crisp and browned, about 25 minutes. (If chicken is not crisp after 20 minutes, increase heat to medium-high.)
3. Of heat, remove pot and carefully flip chicken. Brush skin with za 'atar mixture, transfer skillet to oven, and roast until breast registers 160 degrees and thighs register 175 degrees, 10 to 20 minutes.
4. Transfer chicken to carving board and let rest for 10 minutes. Meanwhile, whisk mint, preserved lemon, vinegar, mustard, ⅛ tsp. salt, and ⅛ tsp. pepper together in bowl until combined. Whisking constantly, slowly drizzle in remaining 3 tbsp. oil until emulsified. Carve chicken and serve with dressing.

CHICKEN TAGINE WITH CHICKPEAS AND APRICOTS

INGREDIENTS FOR 8 SERVINGS:

- 3 (2-inch) strips lemon zest plus 3 tbsp. juice
- 5 garlic cloves, minced
- 4 pounds bone-in chicken pieces (split breasts cut in half, drumsticks, and/or thighs), trimmed
- Salt and pepper
- 2 tbsp. extra-virgin olive oil
- 1 large onion, halved and sliced ¼ inch thick
- 1¼ tsp. paprika
- ½ tsp. ground cumin
- ¼ tsp. cayenne pepper

- ¼ tsp. ground ginger
- ¼ tsp. ground coriander
- ¼ tsp. ground cinnamon
- 2 cups chicken broth
- 2 carrots, peeled, halved lengthwise, and sliced ½ inch thick
- 1 (15-ounce) can chickpeas, rinsed
- 1 tbsp. honey
- 1 cup dried apricots, halved
- 2 tbsp. chopped fresh cilantro

DIRECTIONS:

1. Mince 1 strip lemon zest and combine with 1 tsp. garlic in bowl; set aside.
2. Pat chicken dry with paper towels and season with salt and pepper. Heat oil in Dutch oven over medium-high heat until just smoking. Brown half of chicken well, 5 to 8 minutes per side; transfer to large plate. Repeat with remaining chicken; transfer to plate. Pour of all but 1 tbsp. fat from pot.
3. Add onion and remaining 2 lemon zest strips to fat left in pot and cook over medium heat until softened, about 5 minutes. Stir in remaining garlic, paprika, cumin, cayenne, ginger, coriander, and cinnamon and cook until fragrant, about 1 minute. Stir in broth, scraping up any browned bits. Stir in carrots, chickpeas, and honey and bring to simmer.
4. Nestle chicken into pot along with any accumulated juices and bring to simmer. Reduce heat to medium-low, cover, and cook until breasts register 160 degrees and drumsticks/thighs register 175 degrees, about 20 minutes for breasts and 1 hour for thighs and drumsticks. (If using both types of chicken, simmer thighs and drumsticks for 40 minutes before adding breasts.)
5. Transfer chicken to bowl, tent loosely with aluminum foil, and let rest while finishing sauce. Discard lemon zest. Using large spoon, skim excess fat from surface of sauce. Stir in apricots, return sauce to simmer over medium heat, and cook until apricots are heated through, about 5 minutes. Return chicken and any accumulated juices to pot. Stir in cilantro, lemon juice, and garlic–lemon zest mixture. Season with salt and pepper to taste.

RAISIN STUFFED LAMB

INGREDIENTS FOR 10 SERVINGS:

- 4 pounds lamb shoulder
- 1 tsp. garlic powder
- 1 tsp. onion powder
- 1 tsp. chili powder
- Salt and pepper to taste
- 1 cup golden raisins

- 2 red apples, cored and diced
- 1 tsp. mustard powder
- 1 tsp. cumin powder
- 2 tbsp. pine nuts
- 1 cup dry white wine

DIRECTIONS:

1. Season the lamb with garlic powder, onion powder, chili, salt and pepper.
2. Cut a pocket into the lamb.
3. Mix the raisins, red apples, mustard, cumin and pine nuts and stuff the mixture into the lamb.
4. Place the lamb in a deep dish baking pan and cover with aluminum foil.
5. Cook in the preheated oven at 330F for 2 hours.
6. Serve the lamb warm and fresh.

GRILLED LAMB SHISH KEBABS

 INGREDIENTS FOR 4 SERVINGS:

MARINADE
- 6 tbsp. extra-virgin olive oil
- 7 large fresh mint leaves
- 2 tsp. chopped fresh rosemary
- 2 garlic cloves, peeled

- 1 tsp. salt
- ½ tsp. grated lemon zest plus 2 tbsp. juice
- ¼ tsp. pepper

LAMB AND VEGETABLES
- 2 pounds boneless leg of lamb, pulled apart at seams, trimmed, and cut into 2-inch pieces
- 2 zucchini or yellow summer squash, halved lengthwise and sliced 1 inch thick

- 2 red or green bell peppers, stemmed, seeded, and cut into 1½ -inch pieces 2 red onions, cut into 1-inch pieces, 3 layers thick

 DIRECTIONS:

1. FOR THE MARINADE Process all ingredients in food processor until smooth, about 1 minute, scraping down sides of bowl as needed. Transfer 3 tbsp. marinade to large bowl and set aside.
2. FOR THE LAMB AND VEGETABLES Place remaining marinade and lamb in 1-gallon zipper-lock bag and toss to coat. Press out as much air as possible and seal bag. Refrigerate for at least 1 hour or up to 2 hours, flipping bag every 30 minutes.
3. Add zucchini, bell peppers, and onions to bowl with reserved marinade and toss to coat. Cover and let sit at room temperature for at least 30 minutes.
4. Remove lamb from bag and pat dry with paper towels. Thread lamb tightly onto two 12-inch metal skewers. In alternating pattern of zucchini, bell pepper, and onion, thread vegetables onto four 12-inch metal skewers.
5. 5a. FOR A CHARCOAL GRILL Open bottom vent completely. Light large chimney starter mounded with charcoal briquettes (7 quarts). When top coals are partially covered with ash, pour evenly over center of grill, leaving 2-inch gap between grill wall and charcoal. Set cooking grate in place, cover, and open lid vent completely. Heat grill until hot, about 5 minutes.
6. 5b. FOR A GAS GRILL Turn all burners to high, cover, and heat grill until hot, about 15 minutes. Leave primary burner on high and turn other burner(s) to medium-low.
7. Clean and oil cooking grate. Place lamb skewers on grill (directly over coals if using charcoal or over hotter side of grill if using gas). Place vegetable skewers on grill (near edge of coals but still over coals if using charcoal or on cooler side of grill if using gas). Cook (covered if using gas), turning skewers every 3 to 4 minutes, until lamb is well browned and registers 120 to 125 degrees (for medium-rare), 10 to 15 minutes. Transfer lamb skewers to serving platter, tent loosely with aluminum foil, and let rest while finishing vegetables.
8. Continue to cook vegetable skewers until tender and lightly charred, 5 to 7 minutes; transfer to platter. Using tongs, slide lamb and vegetables of skewers onto platter.

MINTY GRILLED LAMB

 INGREDIENTS FOR 6 SERVINGS:

- 6 lamb chops
- 6 mint leaves, chopped
- 1 cup plain yogurt
- 1 lemon, juiced

- 1 tbsp. lemon zest
- 2 tbsp. olive oil
- Salt and pepper to taste
- Arugula for serving

 DIRECTIONS:

1. Mix all the ingredients in a zip lock bag.
2. Add salt and pepper to taste and place in the fridge for 1 ½ hours.
3. Heat a grill pan over medium flame then place the lamb on the grill.
4. Cook on each side for a few minutes until browned.
5. Serve the chops warm and fresh with arugula.

GREEK-STYLE BRAISED PORK WITH LEEKS

 INGREDIENTS FOR 4 SERVINGS:

- 2 pounds boneless pork butt roast, trimmed and cut into 1-inch pieces Salt and pepper
- 3 tbsp. extra-virgin olive oil
- 2 pounds leeks, white and light green parts only, halved lengthwise, sliced 1 inch thick, and washed thoroughly
- 2 garlic cloves, minced

- 1 (14.5-ounce) can diced tomatoes
- 1 cup dry white wine
- ½ cup chicken broth
- 1 bay leaf
- 2 tsp. chopped fresh oregano

DIRECTIONS:

1. Adjust oven rack to lower-middle position and heat oven to 325 degrees. Pat pork dry with paper towels and season with salt and pepper. Heat 1 tbsp. oil in Dutch oven over medium-high heat until just smoking. Brown half of pork on all sides, about 8 minutes; transfer to bowl. Repeat with 1 tbsp. oil and remaining pork; transfer to bowl.
2. Add remaining 1 tbsp. oil, leeks, ½ tsp. salt, and ½ tsp. pepper to fat left in pot and cook over medium heat, stirring occasionally, until softened and lightly browned, 5 to 7 minutes. Stir in garlic and cook until fragrant, about 30 seconds. Stir in tomatoes and their juice, scraping up any browned bits, and cook until tomato liquid is nearly evaporated, 10 to 12 minutes.
3. Stir in wine, broth, bay leaf, and pork with any accumulated juices and bring to simmer. Cover, transfer pot to oven, and cook until pork is tender and falls apart when prodded with fork, 1 to 1½ hours. Discard bay leaf. Stir in oregano and season with salt and pepper to taste.

CATALAN BRAISED RABBIT

 INGREDIENTS FOR 10 SERVINGS:

- 1 whole rabbit (about 2 ½ pounds), cut into pieces
- 3 tbsp. olive oil
- 4 garlic cloves, chopped
- 1 sweet onion, chopped
- 4 tomatoes, peeled and diced
- ½ cup dry white wine
- 1 cup vegetable stock

- 2 carrots, sliced
- 2 celery stalks, sliced
- 1 thyme sprig
- 1 basil sprig
- ½ cup green olives
- ½ cup kalamata olives
- Salt and pepper to taste

 DIRECTIONS:

1. Heat the oil in a heavy saucepan and stir in the garlic and onion. Cook for 5 minutes then transfer the mix in a deep dish baking pan.
2. Add the rest of the ingredients and season with salt and pepper.
3. Cook in the preheated oven at 350F for 1 hour.
4. Serve the rabbit fresh.

FRIED CHICKEN WITH TZATZIKI SAUCE

 INGREDIENTS FOR 4 SERVINGS:

- 4 chicken breasts, cubed
- 4 tbsp. olive oil
- 1 tsp. dried basil
- 1 tsp. dried oregano
- ½ tsp. chili flakes
- Salt and pepper to taste

- 1 cup Greek yogurt
- 1 cucumber, grated
- 4 garlic cloves, minced
- 1 tsp. lemon juice
- 1 tsp. chopped mint
- 2 tbsp. chopped parsley

 DIRECTIONS:

1. Season the chicken with salt, pepper, basil, oregano and chili.
2. Heat the oil in a skillet and add the chicken. Cook on each side for 5 minutes on high heat just until golden brown.
3. Cover the chicken with a lid and continue cooking for 15-20 more minutes.
4. For the sauce, mix the yogurt, cucumber, garlic, lemon juice, mint and parsley, as well as salt and pepper.
5. Serve the chicken and the sauce fresh.

HONEY ROASTED CHICKEN WITH ROSEMARY POTATOES

INGREDIENTS FOR 8 SERVINGS:

- 1 whole chicken
- 2 tbsp. honey
- 2 tbsp. olive oil
- 1 tsp. cumin powder
- 1 tsp. chili powder
- 1 tsp. dried thyme
- 1 tsp. dried sage

- 1 tsp. smoked paprika
- Salt and pepper
- 2 pounds potatoes, peeled and cubed
- 2 rosemary sprigs
- ¼ cup white wine
- ¼ cup vegetable stock

DIRECTIONS:

1. Mix the honey, oil, spices, herbs, salt and pepper in a bowl.
2. Spread this mixture over the chicken and rub it well into the skin.
3. Place the chicken in a deep dish baking pan.
4. Place the potatoes around the chicken and add the rosemary, wine and stock.
5. Cover with aluminum foil and cook in the preheated oven at 350F for 1 hour then remove the foil and continue cooking for 20 more minutes.
6. Serve the chicken and potatoes warm and fresh.

BRAISED GREEK SAUSAGES WITH PEPPERS

INGREDIENTS FOR 4 SERVINGS:

- 1½ pounds loukaniko sausage
- 2 tbsp. extra-virgin olive oil
- 4 bell peppers (red, yellow, and/or green), stemmed, seeded, and cut into 1½-inch pieces
- 1 onion, chopped
- 2 jalapeño chiles, stemmed, seeded, and minced
- Salt and pepper
- 3 garlic cloves, minced

- 1 tbsp. tomato paste
- 2 tsp. grated orange zest
- 1 tsp. ground fennel
- ½ cup dry white wine
- 1 (14.5-ounce) can diced tomatoes
- ¾ cup chicken broth
- 1 tbsp. minced fresh oregano

DIRECTIONS:

1. Prick sausages with fork in several places. Heat 1 tbsp. oil in 12- inch nonstick skillet over medium-high heat until just smoking. Brown sausages well on all sides, about 8 minutes. Transfer sausages to cutting board, let cool slighty, then cut into quarters.
2. Heat remaining 1 tbsp. oil in now-empty skillet over medium heat until shimmering. Add peppers, onion, jalapeños, ½ tsp. salt, and ½ tsp. pepper and cook until peppers are beginning to soften, about 5 minutes. Stir in garlic, tomato paste, orange zest, and fennel and cook until fragrant, about 1 minute. Stir in wine, scraping up any browned bits.
3. Stir in tomatoes and their juice, broth, and sausages and any accumulated juices and bring to simmer. Cover, reduce heat to low, and simmer gently until sausages are cooked through, about 5 minutes.
4. Uncover, increase heat to medium, and cook until sauce has thickened slightly, about 10 minutes. Stir in oregano and season with salt and pepper to taste.

SPICY, YOGURT-MARINATED CHICKEN SKEWERS

 INGREDIENTS FOR 6 SERVINGS:

- 1 ½ tbsp. Aleppo pepper (extra for garnish)
- 3 tsp. crushed garlic
- 1 tsp. freshly ground black pepper
- 2 tsp. Himalayan salt
- 2 tbsp. tomato paste

- 2 tbsp. balsamic vinegar
- 3 tbsp. extra-virgin olive oil (extra for brushing)
- 1 cup plain Greek yogurt
- 1 ¾ lbs. boneless chicken breasts, skins removed, cubed
- 2 unpeeled lemons, thinly sliced (divided)

DIRECTIONS:

1. Place the Aleppo pepper in a large bowl, along with 1 tbsp. of warm water, and let stand for 5 minutes, until the mixture thickens. Whisk in the garlic, pepper, salt, tomato paste, vinegar, olive oil, and yogurt. Add the chicken cubes, and half of the lemon slices. Toss to coat. Cover the bowl in cling wrap, and chill overnight, or for a minimum of 1 hour.
2. Place 10-12 wooden skewers in a bowl of water, and soak for 20 minutes to prevent charring.
3. Brush a grill with extra olive oil, and heat on medium-high. When the grill is nice and hot. Thread the marinated chicken cubes onto the soaked skewers, discarding the excess marinade. Grill the skewers for 10-12 minutes, turning at regular intervals, until the chicken is cooked all the way through, and nicely browned on all sides.
4. Serve the skewers hot on a bed of lemon slices.

GRILLED CHICKEN WITH GREEK OLIVE RELISH

 INGREDIENTS FOR 4 SERVINGS:

- 4 chicken breasts
- 1 tsp. chili powder
- 1 tsp. cumin powder
- Salt and pepper to taste
- 3 tbsp. olive oil
- 1 cup green olives

- 2 tbsp. chopped parsley
- 1 tbsp. lemon juice
- 1 tsp. lemon zest
- 1 tsp. chopped thyme
- 2 garlic cloves, chopped

DIRECTIONS:

1. Season the chicken with chili powder, cumin, salt and pepper.
2. Heat a grill pan over low to medium flame then drizzle it with oil.
3. Place the chicken on the grill and cook on each side for 10 minutes or until golden brown and the juices are clear.
4. For the relish, mix the olives, parsley, lemon juice, lemon zest, thyme and garlic in a food processor. Pulse until well mixed.
5. Serve the grilled chicken with the olive relish.

CITRUS MARINATED CHICKEN

 INGREDIENTS FOR 8 SERVINGS:

- 8 chicken legs
- 1 orange, sliced
- 1 lemon, sliced
- 1 tbsp. honey
- 1 tsp. sherry vinegar
- 1 tsp. mustard seeds

- 1 tsp. cumin seeds
- 1 tsp. coriander seeds
- 2 tbsp. apricot jam
- 1 bay leaf
- 3 tbsp. olive oil
- Salt and pepper to taste

DIRECTIONS:

1. Combine all the ingredients in a large zip lock bag.
2. Season with salt and pepper and seal well then place in the fridge for 1 ½ hours.
3. Transfer the chicken and the citrus fruits in a deep dish baking pan.
4. Bake in the preheated oven at 350F for 1 ¼ hours.
5. Serve the chicken warm and fresh.

CHAPTER 5: GRAINS/LEGUMES/PASTA

PENNE AND FRESH TOMATO SAUCE WITH SPINACH AND FETA

 INGREDIENTS FOR 6 SERVINGS:

- 3 tbsp. extra-virgin olive oil
- 2 garlic cloves, minced
- 3 pounds ripe tomatoes, cored, peeled, seeded, and cut into ½-inch pieces 5 ounces (5 cups) baby spinach
- 1 pound penne
- Salt and pepper
- 2 tbsp. chopped fresh mint or oregano
- 2 tbsp. lemon juice
- Sugar
- 4 ounces feta cheese, crumbled (1 cup)

DIRECTIONS:

1. Cook 2 tbsp. oil and garlic in 12-inch skillet over medium heat, stirring often, until garlic turns golden but not brown, about 3 minutes. Stir in tomatoes and cook until tomato pieces begin to lose their shape, about 8 minutes. Stir in spinach, 1 handful at a time, and cook until spinach is wilted and tomatoes have made chunky sauce, about 2 minutes.
2. Meanwhile, bring 4 quarts water to boil in large pot. Add pasta and 1 tbsp. salt and cook, stirring often, until al dente. Reserve ½ cup cooking water, then drain pasta and return it to pot.
3. Stir mint, lemon juice, ¼ tsp. salt, and ⅛ tsp. pepper into sauce and season with sugar to taste. Add sauce and remaining 1 tbsp. oil to pasta and toss to combine. Season with salt and pepper to taste and adjust consistency with reserved cooking water as needed. Serve, passing feta separately.

CREAMY GREEN PEA PASTA

 INGREDIENTS FOR 4 SERVINGS:

- 8 oz. whole wheat spaghetti
- 1 cup green peas
- 1 avocado, peeled and cubed
- 2 tbsp. olive oil
- 2 garlic cloves, chopped
- 2 mint leaves
- 1 tbsp. lemon juice
- ¼ cup heavy cream
- 2 tbsp. vegetable stock
- Salt and pepper to taste

 DIRECTIONS:

1. Pour a few cups of water in a deep pot and bring to a boil with a pinch of salt.
2. Add the spaghetti and cook for 8 minutes then drain well.
3. For the sauce, combine the remaining ingredients in a blender and pulse until smooth.
4. Mix the cooked the spaghetti with the sauce and serve the pasta fresh.

ORZO WITH GREEK SAUSAGE AND SPICED YOGURT

 INGREDIENTS FOR 4 SERVINGS:

- 1½ cups orzo
- 1 tbsp. extra-virgin olive oil
- 4 ounces loukaniko sausage, chopped ine
- 1 onion, chopped ine
- 1 red bell pepper, stemmed, seeded, and chopped ine
- 1 tbsp. tomato paste
- 2 garlic cloves, minced
- 1 tsp. paprika
- ¼ tsp. ground cinnamon
- ⅛ tsp. red pepper lakes
- ½ cup dry white wine
- 2½ cups chicken broth
- ¼ cup plain whole-milk Greek yogurt
- 1½ tsp. grated lemon zest
- Salt and pepper
- ¼ cup chopped fresh mint

 DIRECTIONS:

1. Toast orzo in 12-inch skillet over medium-high heat until lightly browned, 3 to 5 minutes; transfer to bowl. Heat oil in now-empty skillet over medium heat until shimmering. Add sausage and cook until browned and fat is rendered, 4 to 6 minutes.
2. Stir in onion and bell pepper and cook until softened, 5 to 7 minutes. Stir in tomato paste, garlic, paprika, cinnamon, and pepper flakes and cook until fragrant, about 1 minute. Stir in wine, scraping up any browned bits. Stir in broth and orzo and bring to simmer. Reduce heat to low, cover, and simmer gently until most of liquid is absorbed, about 10 minutes, stirring once halfway through simmering.
3. Uncover and continue to cook, stirring occasionally, until orzo is aldente and creamy, about 4 minutes. Of heat, stir in yogurt and lemon zest. Season with salt and pepper to taste and adjust consistency with hot water as needed. Sprinkle with mint and serve.

CREAMY PARMESAN POLENTA

 INGREDIENTS FOR 4 SERVINGS:

- 7½ cups water
- Salt and pepper
- Pinch baking soda
- 1½ cups coarse-ground cornmeal
- 2 ounces Parmesan cheese, grated (1 cup), plus extra for serving 2 tbsp. extra-virgin olive oil

 DIRECTIONS:

1. Bring water to boil in large saucepan over medium-high heat. Stir in 1½ tsp. salt and baking soda. Slowly pour cornmeal into water in steady stream while stirring back and forth with wooden spoon or rubber spatula. Bring mixture to boil, stirring constantly, about 1 minute. Reduce heat to lowest setting and cover.
2. After 5 minutes, whisk polenta to smooth out any lumps that may have formed, about 15 seconds. (Make sure to scrape down sides and bottom of saucepan.) Cover and continue to cook, without stirring, until polenta grains are tender but slightly al dente, about 25 minutes longer. (Polenta should be loose and barely hold its shape; it will continue to thicken as it cools.)
3. Of heat, stir in Parmesan and oil and season with pepper to taste. Cover and let sit for 5 minutes. Serve, passing extra Parmesan separately.

WHOLE-WHEAT SPAGHETTI WITH LENTILS, PANCETTA, AND ESCAROLE

INGREDIENTS FOR 6 SERVINGS:

- ¼ cup extra-virgin olive oil
- 4 ounces pancetta, cut into ¼-inch pieces
- 1 onion, chopped ine
- 2 carrots, peeled, halved lengthwise, and sliced ¼ inch thick
- 2 garlic cloves, minced
- ¾ cup lentilles du Puy, picked over and rinsed
- 2 cups chicken broth
- 1½ cups water
- ¼ cup dry white wine
- 1 head escarole (1 pound), trimmed and sliced ½ inch thick
- 1 pound whole-wheat spaghetti
- Salt and pepper
- ¼ cup chopped fresh parsley
- Grated Parmesan cheese

DIRECTIONS:

1. Heat 2 tbsp. oil in large saucepan over medium heat until shimmering. Add pancetta and cook, stirring occasionally, until beginning to brown, 3 to 5 minutes. Add onion and carrots and cook until softened, 5 to 7 minutes. Stir in garlic and cook until fragrant, about 30 seconds. Stir in lentils, broth, and water and bring to simmer. Reduce heat to medium-low, cover, and simmer until lentils are fully cooked and tender, 30 to 40 minutes.

2. Stir in wine and simmer, uncovered, for 2 minutes. Stir in escarole, 1 handful at atime, and cook until completely wilted, about 5 minutes.

3. Meanwhile, bring 4 quarts water to boil in large pot. Add pasta and 1 tbsp. salt and cook, stirring often, until al dente. Reserve ¾ cup cooking water, then drain pasta and return it to pot. Add ½ cup reserved cooking water, lentil mixture, parsley, and remaining 2 tbsp. oil and toss to combine. Season with salt and pepper to taste and adjust consistency with remaining ¼ cup reserved cooking water as needed. Serve with Parmesan.

QUICK TOMATO SAUCE

INGREDIENTS FOR 2 SERVINGS:

- 3 tbsp. extra-virgin olive oil
- 3 garlic cloves, minced
- 1 (28-ounce) can crushed tomatoes
- 1 (14.5-ounce) can diced tomatoes
- 3 tbsp. chopped fresh basil
- ¼ tsp. sugar
- Salt and pepper

DIRECTIONS:

1. Cook oil and garlic in medium saucepan over medium heat, stirring often, until fragrant but not browned, about 2 minutes. Stir in tomatoes and their juice. Bring to simmer and cook until slightly thickened, 15 to 20 minutes. Of heat, stir in basil and sugar. Season with salt and pepper to taste. When tossing sauce with cooked pasta, add some pasta cooking water as needed to adjust consistency.

SPAGHETTI WITH CLAMS AND ROASTED TOMATOES

 INGREDIENTS FOR 6 SERVINGS:

- 2 tbsp. tomato paste
- 3 tbsp. extra-virgin olive oil, plus extra for serving
- 2 tsp. minced fresh thyme or ½ tsp. dried
- Salt and pepper
- 3 pounds ripe tomatoes, cored and halved
- 12 cloves garlic, peeled (8 smashed, 4 minced)
- 1 shallot, sliced thin
- ⅛ tsp. red pepper lakes
- ½ cup dry white wine
- 1 pound spaghetti or linguine
- 4 pounds littleneck clams, scrubbed
- ⅓ cup chopped fresh mint or parsley

 DIRECTIONS:

1. Adjust oven rack to middle position and heat oven to 475 degrees. Combine tomato paste, 1 tbsp. oil, thyme, ¼ tsp. salt, and ¼ tsp. pepper in large bowl. Add tomatoes and smashed garlic and gently toss to coat. Place 4-inch square of aluminum foil in center of wire rack set in rimmed baking sheet lined with aluminum foil. Place smashed garlic cloves on foil and arrange tomatoes, cut side down, around garlic. Roast until tomatoes are soft and skins are well charred, 45 to 55 minutes.

2. Heat remaining 2 tbsp. oil in Dutch oven over medium heat until shimmering. Add shallot, pepper flakes, and minced garlic and cook until fragrant, about 1 minute. Stir in wine and cook until almost completely evaporated, about 1 minute. Stir in roasted tomatoes and garlic and bring to boil. Add clams, cover, and cook, shaking pot occasionally, until clams open, 4 to 8 minutes. As clams open, remove them with slotted spoon and transfer to bowl. Discard any clams that refuse to open. (If desired, remove clams from shells.)

3. Meanwhile, bring 4 quarts water to boil in large pot. Add pasta and 1 tbsp. salt and cook, stirring often, until al dente. Reserve ½ cup cooking water, then drain pasta and add to pot with sauce. Add mint and toss to combine. Season with salt and pepper to taste and adjust consistency with reserved cooking water as needed. Transfer pasta to serving bowl, top with clams, and drizzle with extra oil.

BASMATI RICE PILAF WITH CURRANTS AND TOASTED ALMONDS

 INGREDIENTS FOR 4 SERVINGS:

- 1 tbsp. extra-virgin olive oil
- 1 small onion, chopped ine
- Salt and pepper
- 1½ cups basmati rice, rinsed
- 2 garlic cloves, minced
- ½ tsp. ground turmeric
- ¼ tsp. ground cinnamon
- 2¼ cups water
- ¼ cup currants
- ¼ cup sliced almonds, toasted

DIRECTIONS:

1. Heat oil in large saucepan over medium heat until shimmering. Add onion and ¼ tsp. salt and cook until softened, about 5 minutes. Add rice, garlic, turmeric, and cinnamon and cook, stirring frequently, until grain edges begin to turn translucent, about 3 minutes.

2. Stir in water and bring to simmer. Reduce heat to low, cover, and simmer gently until rice is tender and water is absorbed, 16 to 18 minutes.

3. Of heat, sprinkle currants over pilaf. Cover, laying clean dish towel underneath lid, and let pilafsit for 10 minutes. Add almonds to pilaf and fluf gently with fork to combine. Season with salt and pepper to taste.

SEAFOOD RISOTTO

 INGREDIENTS FOR 4 SERVINGS:

- 12 ounces large shrimp (26 to 30 per pound), peeled and deveined, shells reserved
- 2 cups chicken broth
- 2½ cups water
- 4 (8-ounce) bottles clam juice
- 1 (14.5-ounce) can diced tomatoes, drained
- 2 bay leaves
- 5 tbsp. extra-virgin olive oil
- 1 onion, chopped ine

- 2 cups Arborio rice
- 5 garlic cloves, minced
- 1 tsp. minced fresh thyme or ¼ tsp. dried
- ⅛ tsp. safron threads, crumbled
- 1 cup dry white wine
- 12 ounces small bay scallops
- 2 tbsp. minced fresh parsley
- 1 tbsp. lemon juice
- Salt and pepper

DIRECTIONS:

1. Bring shrimp shells, broth, water, clam juice, tomatoes, and bay leaves to boil in large saucepan over medium-high heat. Reduce to simmer and cook for 20 minutes. Strain mixture through fine-mesh strainer into large bowl, pressing on solids to extract as much liquid as possible; discard solids. Return broth to now-empty saucepan, cover, and keep warm over low heat.
2. Heat 2 tbsp. oil in Dutch oven over medium heat until shimmering. Add onion and cook until softened, about 5 minutes. Add rice, garlic, thyme, and safron and cook, stirring frequently, until grain edges begin to turn translucent, about 3 minutes.
3. Add wine and cook, stirring frequently, until fully absorbed, about 3 minutes. Stir in 3½ cups warm broth, bring to simmer, and cook, stirring occasionally, until almost fully absorbed, 13 to 17 minutes.
4. Continue to cook rice, stirring frequently and adding warm broth, 1 cup at a time, every few minutes as liquid is absorbed, until rice is creamy and cooked through but still somewhat firm in center, 13 to 17 minutes.
5. Stir in shrimp and scallops and cook, stirring frequently, until opaque throughout, about 3 minutes. Remove pot from heat, cover, and let sit for 5 minutes. Adjust consistency with remaining warm broth as needed (you may have broth left over). Stir in remaining 3 tbsp. oil, parsley, and lemon juice and season with salt and pepper to taste.

STOVETOP WHITE RICE

 INGREDIENTS FOR 4 SERVINGS:

- 1 tbsp. extra-virgin olive oil
- 2 cups long-grain white rice, rinsed

- 3 cups water
- Salt and pepper

DIRECTIONS:

1. Heat oil in large saucepan over medium heat until shimmering. Add rice and cook, stirring often, until grain edges begin to turn translucent, about 2 minutes. Add water and 1 tsp. salt and bring to simmer. Cover, reduce heat to low, and simmer gently until rice is tender and water is absorbed, about 20 minutes. Of heat, lay clean dish towel underneath lid and let rice sit for 10 minutes. Gently luf rice with fork. Season with salt and pepper to taste.

WARM FARRO WITH LEMON AND HERBS

 INGREDIENTS FOR 4 SERVINGS:

- 1½ cups whole farro
- Salt and pepper
- 3 tbsp. extra-virgin olive oil
- 1 onion, chopped ine

- 1 garlic clove, minced
- ¼ cup chopped fresh parsley
- ¼ cup chopped fresh mint
- 1 tbsp. lemon juice

DIRECTIONS:

1. Bring 4 quarts water to boil in Dutch oven. Add farro and 1 tbsp. salt, return to boil, and cook until grains are tender with slight chew, 15 to 30 minutes. Drain farro, return to now-empty pot, and cover to keep warm.
2. Heat 2 tbsp. oil in 12-inch skillet over medium heat until shimmering. Add onion and ¼ tsp. salt and cook until softened, about 5 minutes. Stir in garlic and cook until fragrant, about 30 seconds.
3. Add remaining 1 tbsp. oil and farro and cook, stirring frequently, until heated through, about 2 minutes. Of heat, stir in parsley, mint, and lemon juice. Season with salt and pepper to taste.

COUSCOUS WITH LAMB, CHICKPEAS, AND ORANGE

 INGREDIENTS FOR 6 SERVINGS:

- 3 tbsp. extra-virgin olive oil, plus extra for serving
- 1½ cups couscous
- 1 pound lamb shoulder chops (blade or round bone), 1 to 1½ inches thick, trimmed and halved
- Salt and pepper
- 1 onion, chopped ine
- 10 (2-inch) strips orange zest (1 orange)
- 1 tsp. grated fresh ginger
- 1 tsp. ground coriander

- ¼ tsp. ground cinnamon
- ⅛ tsp. cayenne pepper
- ½ cup dry white wine
- 2½ cups chicken broth
- 1 (15-ounce) can chickpeas, rinsed
- ½ cup raisins
- ½ cup sliced almonds, toasted
- ⅓ cup minced fresh parsley

 DIRECTIONS:

1. Adjust oven rack to lower-middle position and heat oven to 325 degrees. Heat 2 tbsp. oil in Dutch oven over medium-high heat until shimmering. Add couscous and cook, stirring frequently, until grains are just beginning to brown, 3 to 5 minutes. Transfer to bowl and wipe pot clean with paper towels.
2. Pat lamb dry with paper towels and season with salt and pepper. Heat remaining 1 tbsp. oil in now-empty pot over medium-high heat until just smoking. Brown lamb, about 4 minutes per side; transfer to plate.
3. Add onion to fat left in pot and cook over medium heat until softened, about 5 minutes. Stir in orange zest, ginger, coriander, cinnamon, cayenne, and ⅛ tsp. pepper and cook until fragrant, about 30 seconds. Stir in wine, scraping up any browned bits. Stir in broth and chickpeas and bring to boil.
4. Nestle lamb into pot along with any accumulated juices. Cover, place pot in oven, and cook until fork slips easily in and out of lamb, about 1 hour.
5. Transfer lamb to cutting board, let cool slightly, then shred into bite-size pieces using 2 forks, discarding excess fat and bones. Strain cooking liquid through fine mesh strainer set over bowl. Return solids and 1½ cups cooking liquid to now-empty pot and bring to simmer over medium heat; discard remaining liquid.
6. Stir in couscous and raisins. Cover, remove pot from heat, and let sit until couscous is tender, about 7 minutes. Add shredded lamb, almonds, and parsley to couscous and gently fluf with fork to combine. Season with salt and pepper to taste and drizzle with extra oil.

CREAMY PARMESAN POLENTA

 INGREDIENTS FOR 4 SERVINGS:

- 7½ cups water
- Salt and pepper
- Pinch baking soda
- 1½ cups coarse-ground cornmeal
- 2 ounces Parmesan cheese, grated (1 cup), plus extra for serving 2 tbsp. extra-virgin olive oil

DIRECTIONS:

1. Bring water to boil in large saucepan over medium-high heat. Stir in 1½ tsp. salt and baking soda. Slowly pour cornmeal into water in steady stream while stirring back and forth with wooden spoon or rubber spatula. Bring mixture to boil, stirring constantly, about 1 minute. Reduce heat to lowest setting and cover.
2. After 5 minutes, whisk polenta to smooth out any lumps that may have formed, about 15 seconds. (Make sure to scrape down sides and bottom of saucepan.) Cover and continue to cook, without stirring, until polenta grains are tender but slightly al dente, about 25 minutes longer. (Polenta should be loose and barely hold its shape; it will continue to thicken as it cools.)
3. Of heat, stir in Parmesan and oil and season with pepper to taste. Cover and let sit for 5 minutes. Serve, passing extra Parmesan separately.

BULGUR SALAD WITH CARROTS AND ALMONDS

INGREDIENTS FOR 4 SERVINGS:

- 1½ cups medium-grind bulgur, rinsed
- 1 cup water
- 6 tbsp. lemon juice (2 lemons)
- Salt and pepper
- ⅓ cup extra-virgin olive oil
- ½ tsp. ground cumin

- ⅛ tsp. cayenne pepper
- 4 carrots, peeled and shredded
- 3 scallions, sliced thin
- ½ cup sliced almonds, toasted
- ⅓ cup chopped fresh mint
- ⅓ cup chopped fresh cilantro

DIRECTIONS:

1. Combine bulgur, water, ¼ cup lemon juice, and ¼ tsp. salt in bowl. Cover and let sit at room temperature until grains are softened and liquid is fully absorbed, about 1½ hours.
2. Whisk remaining 2 tbsp. lemon juice, oil, cumin, cayenne, and ½ tsp. salt together in large bowl. Add bulgur, carrots, scallions, almonds, mint, and cilantro and gently toss to combine. Season with salt and pepper to taste.

WARM FARRO WITH FENNEL AND PARMESAN

INGREDIENTS FOR 4 SERVINGS:

- 1½ cups whole farro
- Salt and pepper
- 3 tbsp. extra-virgin olive oil
- 1 onion, chopped ine
- 1 small fennel bulb, stalks discarded, bulb halved, cored, and chopped ine 3 garlic cloves, minced

- 1 tsp. minced fresh thyme or ¼ tsp. dried
- 1 ounce Parmesan cheese, grated (½ cup)
- ¼ cup minced fresh parsley
- 2 tsp. sherry vinegar

DIRECTIONS:

1. Bring 4 quarts water to boil in Dutch oven. Add farro and 1 tbsp. salt, return to boil, and cook until grains are tender with slight chew, 15 to 30 minutes. Drain farro, return to now-empty pot, and cover to keep warm.
2. Heat 2 tbsp. oil in 12-inch skillet over medium heat until shimmering. Add onion, fennel, and ¼ tsp. salt and cook, stirring occasionally, until softened, 8 to 10 minutes. Add garlic and thyme and cook until fragrant, about 30 seconds.
3. Add remaining 1 tbsp. oil and farro and cook, stirring frequently, until heated through, about 2 minutes. Of heat, stir in Parmesan, parsley, and vinegar. Season with salt and pepper to taste.

FRENCH LENTILS WITH CARROTS AND PARSLEY

INGREDIENTS FOR 4 SERVINGS:

- 2 carrots, peeled and chopped ine
- 1 onion, chopped ine
- 1 celery rib, chopped ine
- 2 tbsp. extra-virgin olive oil
- Salt and pepper
- 2 garlic cloves, minced

- 1 tsp. minced fresh thyme or ¼ tsp. dried
- 2½ cups water
- 1 cup lentilles du Puy, picked over and rinsed
- 2 tbsp. minced fresh parsley
- 2 tsp. lemon juice

DIRECTIONS:

1. Combine carrots, onion, celery, 1 tbsp. oil, and ½ tsp. salt in large saucepan. Cover and cook over medium-low heat, stirring occasionally, until vegetables are softened, 8 to 10 minutes. Stir in garlic and thyme and cook until fragrant, about 30 seconds.
2. Stir in water and lentils and bring to simmer. Reduce heat to low, cover, and simmer gently, stirring occasionally, until lentils are mostly tender, 40 to 50 minutes.
3. Uncover and continue to cook, stirring occasionally, until lentils are completely tender, about 8 minutes. Stir in remaining 1 tbsp. oil, parsley, and lemon juice. Season with salt and pepper to taste and serve.

CHICKPEAS WITH GARLIC AND PARSLEY

 INGREDIENTS FOR 6 SERVINGS:

- ¼ cup extra-virgin olive oil
- 4 garlic cloves, sliced thin
- ⅛ tsp. red pepper lakes
- 1 onion, chopped ine
- Salt and pepper

- 2 (15-ounce) cans chickpeas, rinsed
- 1 cup chicken or vegetable broth
- 2 tbsp. minced fresh parsley
- 2 tsp. lemon juice

DIRECTIONS:

1. Cook 3 tbsp. oil, garlic, and pepper flakes in 12-inch skillet over medium heat, stirring frequently, until garlic turns golden but not brown, about 3 minutes. Stir in onion and ¼ tsp. salt and cook until softened and lightly browned, 5 to 7 minutes. Stir in chickpeas and broth and bring to simmer. Reduce heat to medium-low, cover, and cook until chickpeas are heated through and flavors meld, about 7 minutes.
2. Uncover, increase heat to high, and continue to cook until nearly all liquid has evaporated, about 3 minutes. Of heat, stir in parsley and lemon juice. Season with salt and pepper to taste and drizzle with remaining 1 tbsp. oil.

CRANBERRY BEANS WITH WARM SPICES

 INGREDIENTS FOR 6 SERVINGS:

- Salt and pepper
- 1 pound (2½ cups) dried cranberry beans, picked over and rinsed ¼ cup extra-virgin olive oil
- 1 onion, chopped ine
- 2 carrots, peeled and chopped ine
- 4 garlic cloves, sliced thin

- 1 tbsp. tomato paste
- ½ tsp. ground cinnamon
- ½ cup dry white wine
- 4 cups chicken or vegetable broth
- 2 tbsp. lemon juice, plus extra for seasoning
- 2 tbsp. minced fresh mint

DIRECTIONS:

1. Dissolve 3 tbsp. salt in 4 quarts cold water in large container. Add beans and soak at room temperature for at least 8 hours or up to 24 hours. Drain and rinse well.
2. Adjust oven rack to lower-middle position and heat oven to 350 degrees. Heat oil in Dutch oven over medium heat until shimmering. Add onion and carrots and cook until softened, about 5 minutes. Stir in garlic, tomato paste, cinnamon, and ¼ tsp. pepper and cook until fragrant, about 1 minute. Stir in wine, scraping up any browned bits. Stir in broth, ½ cup water, and beans and bring to boil. Cover, transfer pot to oven, and cook until beans are tender, about 1½ hours, stirring every 30 minutes.
3. Stir in lemon juice and mint. Season with salt, pepper, and extra lemon juice to taste. Adjust consistency with extra hot water as needed.

SIMPLE COUSCOUS

 INGREDIENTS FOR 6 SERVINGS:

- 2 tbsp. extra-virgin olive oil
- 2 cups couscous
- 1 cup water

- 1 cup chicken or vegetable broth
- Salt and pepper

 DIRECTIONS:

1. Heat oil in medium saucepan over medium-high heat until shimmering. Add couscous and cook, stirring frequently, until grains are just beginning to brown, 3 to 5 minutes. Stir in water, broth, and 1 tsp. salt. Cover, remove saucepan from heat, and let sit until couscous is tender, about 7 minutes. Gently fluf couscous with fork and season with pepper to taste.

PENNE WITH ROASTED CHERRY TOMATO SAUCE

 INGREDIENTS FOR 6 SERVINGS:

- 1 shallot, sliced thin
- ¼ cup extra-virgin olive oil
- 2 pounds cherry tomatoes, halved
- 3 large garlic cloves, sliced thin
- 1 tbsp. balsamic vinegar
- 1½ tsp. sugar, or to taste

- Salt and pepper
- ¼ tsp. red pepper lakes
- 1 pound penne
- ¼ cup coarsely chopped fresh basil
- Grated Parmesan cheese

 DIRECTIONS:

1. Adjust oven rack to middle position and heat oven to 350 degrees. Toss shallot with 1 tsp. oil in bowl. In separate bowl, gently toss tomatoes with remaining oil, garlic, vinegar, sugar, ½ tsp. salt, ¼ tsp. pepper, and pepper flakes. Spread tomato mixture in even layer in rimmed baking sheet, scatter shallot over tomatoes, and roast until edges of shallot begin to brown and tomato skins are slightly shriveled, 35 to 40 minutes. (Do not stir tomatoes during roasting.) Let cool for 5 to 10 minutes.
2. Meanwhile, bring 4 quarts water to boil in large pot. Add pasta and 1 tbsp. salt and cook, stirring often, until al dente. Reserve ½ cup cooking water, then drain pasta and return it to pot. Using rubber spatula, scrape tomato mixture onto pasta. Add basil and toss to combine. Season with salt and pepper to taste and adjust consistency with reserved cooking water as needed. Serve with Parmesan.

TAGLIATELLE WITH ARTICHOKES AND PARMESAN

 INGREDIENTS FOR 6 SERVINGS:

- 4 cups jarred whole baby artichoke hearts packed in water
- ¼ cup extra-virgin olive oil, plus extra for serving
- Salt and pepper
- 4 garlic cloves, minced
- 2 anchovy illets, rinsed, patted dry, and minced
- 1 tbsp. minced fresh oregano or 1 tsp. dried

- ¼–½ tsp. red pepper lakes
- ½ cup dry white wine
- 1 pound tagliatelle
- 1 ounce Parmesan cheese, grated (½ cup), plus extra for serving ¼ cup minced fresh parsley
- 1½ tsp. grated lemon zest
- 1 recipe Parmesan Bread Crumbs

DIRECTIONS:

1. Cut leaves from artichoke hearts. Cut hearts in half and dry with paper towels. Place leaves in bowl and cover with water. Let leaves sit for 15 minutes. Drain well.
2. Heat 1 tbsp. oil in 12-inch nonstick skillet over medium-high heat until shimmering. Add artichoke hearts and ⅛ tsp. salt and cook, stirring frequently, until spotty brown, 7 to 9 minutes. Stir in garlic, anchovies, oregano, and pepper flakes and cook, stirring constantly, until fragrant, about 30 seconds. Stir in wine and bring to simmer. Of heat, stir in artichoke leaves.
   Meanwhile, bring 4 quarts water to boil in large pot. Add pasta and 1 tbsp. salt and cook, stirring often, until al dente. Reserve 1½ cups cooking water, then drain pasta and return it to pot. Add 1 cup reserved cooking water, artichoke mixture, Parmesan, parsley, lemon zest, and remaining 3 tbsp. oil and toss to combine. Season with salt and pepper to taste and adjust consistency with remaining ½ cup reserved cooking water as needed. Serve, sprinkling individual portions with bread crumbs and extra Parmesan and drizzling with extra oil.

CHAPTER 6: SOUP/STEWS

WHITE GAZPACHO

 INGREDIENTS FOR 8 SERVINGS:

- 6 slices hearty white sandwich bread, crusts removed
- 4 cups water
- 2½ cups (8¾ ounces) plus ⅓ cup sliced blanched almonds
- 1 garlic clove, peeled and smashed
- 3 tbsp. sherry vinegar
- Salt and pepper
- Pinch cayenne pepper
- ½ cup plus 2 tsp. extra-virgin olive oil, plus extra for serving ½ tsp. almond extract
- 6 ounces seedless green grapes, sliced thin (1 cup)

DIRECTIONS:

1. Combine bread and water in bowl and let soak for 5 minutes. Process 2½ cups almonds in blender until finely ground, about 30 seconds, scraping down sides of blender jar as needed. Using your hands, remove bread from water, squeeze it lightly, and transfer to blender with almonds. Measure out 3 cups soaking water and set aside; transfer remaining soaking water to blender. Add garlic, vinegar, ½ tsp. salt, and cayenne to blender and process until mixture has consistency of cake batter, 30 to 45 seconds. With blender running, add ½ cup oil in thin, steady stream, about 30 seconds. Add reserved soaking water and process for 1 minute.
2. Season soup with salt and pepper to taste, then strain through fine-mesh strainer into bowl, pressing on solids to extract as much liquid as possible; discard solids.
3. Transfer 1 tbsp. soup to separate bowl and stir in almond extract. Return 1 tsp. extract-soup mixture to soup; discard remaining mixture. Cover and refrigerate to blend flavors, at least 4 hours or up to 24 hours.
4. Heat remaining 2 tsp. oil in 8-inch skillet over medium-high heat until shimmering. Add remaining ⅓ cup almonds and cook, stirring constantly, until golden brown, 3 to 4 minutes. Immediately transfer almonds to bowl, stir in ¼ tsp. salt, and let cool slightly.
5. Ladle soup into shallow bowls. Mound grapes in center of each bowl, sprinkle with almonds, and drizzle with extra oil. Serve immediately.

MEDITERRANEAN SAUSAGE SOUP

 INGREDIENTS FOR 8 SERVINGS:

- 2 tbsp. olive oil
- 4 chicken sausages, halved
- 2 shallots, chopped
- 1 garlic clove, chopped
- 2 red bell peppers, cored and diced
- 1 zucchini, cubed
- 2 cups cauliflower florets
- 1 can diced tomatoes
- 2 cups vegetable stock
- 6 cups water
- Salt and pepper to taste
- ½ tsp. dried oregano
- ½ tsp. dried basil
- ½ tsp. dried thyme

DIRECTIONS:

1. Heat the oil in a soup pot and stir in the sausages. Cook for 5 minutes then stir in the rest of the ingredients.
2. Add salt and pepper to taste and cook on low heat for 25 minutes.
3. Serve the soup warm and fresh.

ROASTED EGGPLANT AND TOMATO SOUP

👥 INGREDIENTS FOR 4 SERVINGS:

- 2 pounds eggplant, cut into ½-inch pieces
- 6 tbsp. extra-virgin olive oil, plus extra for serving
- 1 onion, chopped
- Salt and pepper
- 2 garlic cloves, minced
- 1½ tsp. ras el hanout
- ½ tsp. ground cumin
- 4 cups chicken or vegetable broth, plus extra as needed
- 1 (14.5-ounce) can diced tomatoes, drained
- ¼ cup raisins
- 1 bay leaf
- 2 tsp. lemon juice
- 2 tbsp. slivered almonds, toasted
- 2 tbsp. minced fresh cilantro

⚙ DIRECTIONS:

1. Adjust oven rack 4 inches from broiler element and heat broiler. Toss eggplant with 5 tbsp. oil, then spread in aluminum foil–lined rimmed baking sheet. Broil eggplant for 10 minutes. Stir eggplant and continue to broil until mahogany brown, 5 to 7 minutes. Measure out and reserve 2 cups eggplant.
2. Heat remaining 1 tbsp. oil in large saucepan over medium heat until shimmering. Add onion, ¾ tsp. salt, and ¼ tsp. pepper and cook until softened and lightly browned, 5 to 7 minutes. Stir in garlic, ras el hanout, and cumin and cook until fragrant, about 30 seconds. Stir in broth, tomatoes, raisins, bay leaf, and remaining eggplant and bring to simmer. Reduce heat to low, cover, and simmer gently until eggplant is softened, about 20 minutes.
3. Discard bay leaf. Working in batches, process soup in blender until smooth, about 2 minutes. Return soup to clean saucepan and stir in reserved eggplant. Heat soup gently over low heat until hot (do not boil) and adjust consistency with extra hot broth as needed. Stir in lemon juice and season with salt and pepper to taste. Serve, sprinkling individual portions with almonds and cilantro and drizzling with extra oil.

PAPRIKA STEWED LAMB

👥 INGREDIENTS FOR 8 SERVINGS:

- 3 tbsp. olive oil
- 2 pounds lamb shoulder, cubed
- 1 tsp. smoked paprika
- 1 tsp. cumin powder
- 1 tsp. chili powder
- 1 bay leaf

- 1 bay leaf
- 1 sage leaf
- 1 can diced tomatoes
- 1 cup dry red wine
- Salt and pepper to taste

⚙ DIRECTIONS:

1. Season the lamb with salt, pepper, paprika, cumin and chili powder.
2. Heat the oil in a skillet and stir in the lamb. Cook for 5 minutes then add the rest of the ingredients.
3. Cook on low heat for 1 ¼ hours.
4. Serve the lamb and the sauce warm and fresh.

SPANISH-STYLE LENTIL AND CHORIZO SOUP

INGREDIENTS FOR 6 SERVINGS:

- 1 pound (2¼ cups) lentils, picked over and rinsed
- Salt and pepper
- 1 large onion
- 5 tbsp. extra-virgin olive oil
- 1½ pounds Spanish-style chorizo sausage, pricked with fork several times
- 3 carrots, peeled and cut into ¼-inch pieces
- 3 tbsp. minced fresh parsley
- 3 tbsp. sherry vinegar, plus extra for seasoning
- 2 bay leaves
- ⅛ tsp. ground cloves
- 2 tbsp. sweet smoked paprika
- 3 garlic cloves, minced
- 1 tbsp. all-purpose lour

DIRECTIONS:

1. Place lentils and 2 tsp. salt in heatproof container. Cover with 4 cups boiling water and let soak for 30 minutes. Drain well.

2. Meanwhile, finely chop three-quarters of onion (you should have about 1 cup) and grate remaining quarter (you should have about 3 tbsp.). Heat 2 tbsp. oil in Dutch oven over medium heat until shimmering. Add chorizo and cook until browned on all sides, 6 to 8 minutes. Transfer chorizo to large plate. Reduce heat to low and add chopped onion, carrots, 1 tbsp. parsley, and 1 tsp. salt. Cover and cook, stirring occasionally, until vegetables are very soft but not brown, 25 to 30 minutes. If vegetables begin to brown, add 1 tbsp. water to pot.

3. Add lentils and vinegar to vegetables, increase heat to medium-high, and cook, stirring frequently, until vinegar starts to evaporate, 3 to 4 minutes. Add 7 cups water, chorizo, bay leaves, and cloves; bring to simmer. Reduce heat to low; cover; and cook until lentils are tender, about 30 minutes.

4. Heat remaining 3 tbsp. oil in small saucepan over medium heat until shimmering. Add paprika, grated onion, garlic, and ½ tsp. pepper; cook, stirring constantly, until fragrant, 2 minutes. Add flour and cook, stirring constantly, 1 minute longer. Remove chorizo and bay leaves from lentils. Stir paprika mixture into lentils and continue to cook until flavors have blended and soup has thickened, 10 to 15 minutes. When chorizo is cool enough to handle, cut in half lengthwise, then cut each half into ¼-inch-thick slices. Return chorizo to soup along with remaining 2 tbsp. parsley and heat through, about 1 minute. Season with salt, pepper, and up to 2 tsp. vinegar to taste and serve. (Soup can be made up to 3 days in advance.)

REDWINE BRAISED BEEF STEW

 INGREDIENTS FOR 4 SERVINGS:

- 1 tbsp. extra-virgin avocado oil
- 1 lb. beef stew meat, cut into bite-sized pieces
- 8 oz. button mushrooms, diced
- 3 tbsp. tomato paste
- ½ cup dry red wine
- 3 ½ cups beef stock (divided)
- 1 tsp. Italian seasoning
- 2 tsp. crushed garlic

- 1 medium carrot, sliced into half-moons
- ½ medium shallot, diced
- 2 medium russet potatoes, diced
- ¼ tsp. kosher salt
- White pepper
- 1 tsp. arrowroot
- Fresh chives, chopped

DIRECTIONS:

1. In a large pot over medium-high heat, heat the oil. When the oil is nice and hot, scrape the beef cubes into it, and fry for about 5 minutes, or until the cubes are nicely browned on all sides. Add the mushrooms, and fry for an additional 5 minutes until the mushrooms darken in color. Stir in the tomato paste for 1 minute. Add the wine to the pot, and bring to a gentle boil, scraping up any bits of food that may have stuck to the bottom of the pot. When the wine has reduced by half, add 3 ¼ cups of the beef stock to the pot, stirring to combine.
2. Stir in the Italian seasoning, garlic, carrots, shallots, potatoes, salt, and a generous pinch of pepper. Allow the stew to gently simmer for about 25 minutes, or until the vegetables are fork-tender, stirring occasionally.
3. In a medium-sized bowl, whisk the arrowroot with the remaining beef stock, until dissolved. Whisk the mixture into the stew, and simmer for an additional 5 minutes.
4. Ladle the stew into bowls, and serve hot, garnished with the fresh chives.

ITALIAN BEAN & CABBAGE SOUP

 INGREDIENTS FOR 6 SERVINGS:

- 4 cups chicken broth
- 6 oz. canned tomato paste
- ½ tsp. Himalayan salt
- 1 whole bay leaf
- 2 fresh thyme sprigs
- 2 tsp. crushed garlic
- 15.5 oz. white beans, drained and rinsed

- 1 small shallot, chopped
- 2 large carrots, chopped
- 4 celery stalks, chopped
- 1 ½ lbs. cabbage, shredded
- Parmesan cheese, grated, for garnish

 DIRECTIONS:

1. In a large slow cooker, whisk together the chicken broth and tomato paste, until properly combined. Stir in the salt, bay leaf, thyme sprigs, garlic, beans, shallots, carrots, celery, and cabbage, until all of the ingredients are properly combined. Place the lid on the slow cooker, and cook on low for 6-8 hours, until the vegetables are fork-tender.
2. Discard the bay leaf and thyme sprigs. Spoon the soup into bowls, and serve hot, garnished with parmesan.

SPINACH ORZO SOUP

 INGREDIENTS FOR 8 SERVINGS:

- 2 tbsp. extra virgin olive oil
- 2 shallots, chopped
- 2 garlic cloves, chopped
- 1 green bell pepper, cored and diced
- 1 yellow bell pepper, cored and diced
- 4 cups baby spinach

- 1 cup green peas
- 2 cups vegetable stock
- 4 cups water
- 2 tbsp. lemon juice
- Salt and pepper to taste
- ¼ cup orzo

DIRECTIONS:

1. Heat the oil in a soup pot and stir in the shallots and garlic.
2. Cook for 2 minutes then add the rest of the ingredients and season with salt and pepper.
3. Cook on low heat for 25 minutes.
4. Serve the soup warm or chilled.

CREAMY ROASTED VEGETABLE SOUP

 INGREDIENTS FOR 8 SERVINGS:

- 2 red onions, sliced
- 1 zucchini, sliced
- 2 tomatoes, sliced
- 2 potatoes, sliced
- 2 garlic cloves
- 2 tbsp. olive oil
- 1 tsp. dried basil

- 1 tsp. dried oregano
- 4 cups vegetable stock
- 8 cups water
- Salt and pepper to taste
- 1 bay leaf
- 1 thyme sprig

DIRECTIONS:

1. Combine the onions, zucchini, tomatoes, potatoes, garlic, oil, basil and oregano in a deep dish baking pan.
2. Season with salt and pepper and cook in the preheated oven at 400F for 30 minutes or until golden brown.
3. Transfer the vegetables in a soup pot and add the stock and water.
4. Stir in the bay leaf and thyme sprig and cook for 15 minutes.
5. When done, remove the thyme and bay leaf and puree the soup with an immersion blender.
6. Serve the soup warm and fresh.

FIG LAMB STEW

 INGREDIENTS FOR 8 SERVINGS:

- 3 tbsp. olive oil
- 2 pounds lamb shoulder, cubed
- 2 shallots, chopped
- 4 garlic cloves, chopped
- 2 celery stalks, sliced
- 2 carrots, sliced
- 1 can diced tomatoes

- 1 cup vegetable stock
- 1 rosemary sprig
- Salt and pepper to taste
- 1 pound fresh figs, halved
- 4 oz. goat cheese, crumbled
- 2 tbsp. chopped parsley

 DIRECTIONS:

1. Heat the oil in a skillet and stir in the lamb.
2. Cook for 5 minutes on each side then add the shallots, garlic, celery, carrots, tomatoes, stock and rosemary, as well as salt and pepper.
3. Cook on low heat with a lid on for 30 minutes then add the figs and continue cooking for another 10 minutes.
4. Serve the stew warm and fresh, topped with cheese and parsley.

CHILLED CUCUMBER AND YOGURT SOUP

INGREDIENTS FOR 6 SERVINGS:

- 5 pounds English cucumbers, peeled and seeded (1 cucumber cut into ½-inch pieces, remaining cucumbers cut into 2-inch pieces)
- 4 scallions, green parts only, chopped coarse
- 2 cups water
- 2 cups plain Greek yogurt
- 1 tbsp. lemon juice
- Salt and pepper
- ¼ tsp. sugar
- 1½ tbsp. minced fresh dill
- 1½ tbsp. minced fresh mint
- Extra-virgin olive oil

DIRECTIONS:

1. Toss 2-inch pieces of cucumber with scallions. Working in 2 batches, process cucumber-scallion mixture in blender with water until completely smooth, about 2 minutes; transfer to large bowl. Whisk in yogurt, lemon juice, 1½ tsp. salt, sugar, and pinch pepper. Cover and refrigerate to blend flavors, at least 1 hour or up to 12 hours.
2. Stir in dill and mint and season with salt and pepper to taste. Serve, topping individual portions with remaining ½-inch pieces of cucumber and drizzling with oil.

TURKISH TOMATO, BULGUR, AND RED PEPPER SOUP

INGREDIENTS FOR 6 SERVINGS:

- 2 tbsp. extra-virgin olive oil
- 1 onion, chopped
- 2 red bell peppers, stemmed, seeded, and chopped
- Salt and pepper
- 3 garlic cloves, minced
- 1 tsp. dried mint, crumbled
- ½ tsp. smoked paprika
- ⅛ tsp. red pepper lakes
- 1 tbsp. tomato paste
- ½ cup dry white wine
- 1 (28-ounce) can diced ire-roasted tomatoes
- 4 cups chicken or vegetable broth
- 2 cups water
- ¾ cup medium-grind bulgur, rinsed
- ⅓ cup chopped fresh mint

DIRECTIONS:

1. Heat oil in Dutch oven over medium heat until shimmering. Add onion, bell peppers, ¾ tsp. salt, and ¼ tsp. pepper and cook until softened and lightly browned, 6 to 8 minutes. Stir in garlic, dried mint, smoked paprika, and pepper flakes and cook until fragrant, about 30 seconds. Stir in tomato paste and cook for 1 minute.
2. Stir in wine, scraping up any browned bits, and simmer until reduced by half, about 1 minute. Add tomatoes and their juice and cook, stirring occasionally, unti tomatoes soften and begin to break apart, about 10 minutes.
3. Stir in broth, water, and bulgur and bring to simmer. Reduce heat to low, cover, and simmer gently until bulgur is tender, about 20 minutes. Season with salt and pepper to taste. Serve, sprinkling individual portions with fresh mint.

SWEET AND SOUR RHUBARB LENTIL SOUP

INGREDIENTS FOR 6 SERVINGS:

- 2 tbsp. olive oil
- 1 shallot, chopped
- 1 garlic clove, chopped
- 1 green bell pepper, cored and diced
- 1 yellow bell pepper, cored and diced
- 1 carrot, diced
- 1 celery stalk, diced
- 1 cup green lentils
- 4 rhubarbstalks, sliced
- 2 cups vegetable stock
- 6 cups water
- ½ cup diced tomatoes
- Salt and pepper to taste
- 1 thyme sprig
- 1 oregano sprig

DIRECTIONS:

1. Heat the oil in a soup pot and stir in the shallot, garlic, bell peppers, carrot and celery.
2. Cook for 5 minutes until softened then add the lentils, rhubarb, stock and water, as well as tomatoes.
3. Season with salt and pepper and add the thyme and oregano sprig.
4. Cook on low heat for 20 minutes.
5. Serve the soup warm or chilled.

MOROCCAN-STYLE CHICKPEA SOUP

 INGREDIENTS FOR 6 SERVINGS:

- 3 tbsp. extra-virgin olive oil
- 1 onion, chopped ine
- 1 tsp. sugar
- Salt and pepper
- 4 garlic cloves, minced
- ½ tsp. hot paprika
- ¼ tsp. safron threads, crumbled
- ¼ tsp. ground ginger

- ¼ tsp. ground cumin
- 2 (15-ounce) cans chickpeas, rinsed
- 1 pound red potatoes, unpeeled, cut into ½-inch pieces
- 1 (14.5-ounce) can diced tomatoes
- 1 zucchini, cut into ½-inch pieces
- 3½ cups chicken or vegetable broth
- ¼ cup minced fresh parsley or mint
- Lemon wedges

DIRECTIONS:

1. Heat oil in Dutch oven over medium-high heat until shimmering. Add onion, sugar, and ½ tsp. salt and cook until onion is softened, about 5 minutes. Stir in garlic, paprika, safron, ginger, and cumin and cook until fragrant, about 30 seconds. Stir in chickpeas, potatoes, tomatoes and their juice, zucchini, and broth. Bring to simmer and cook, stirring occasionally, until potatoes are tender, 20 to 30 minutes.
2. Using wooden spoon, mash some of potatoes against side of pot to thicken soup. Of heat, stir in parsley and season with salt and pepper to taste. Serve with lemon wedges.

DELICIOUS CHICKPEA & PASTA SOUP

 INGREDIENTS FOR 4 SERVINGS:

- 15 oz. canned chickpeas, drained and rinsed
- 4 cups chicken stock
- pinch of saffron
- 1 tsp. kosher salt
- ⅓ cup avocado oil
- 6 oz. farfalle pasta, cooked according to package instructions, and thoroughly drained

DIRECTIONS:

1. Bring the chickpeas and stock to a boil in a large pot over medium-high heat. Lower the heat, and simmer for 10 minutes until the chickpeas have softened, stirring at regular intervals to prevent burning. Add the saffron and salt, stirring to incorporate.
2. While the soup simmers, add the avocado oil to a large frying pan, and heat over medium-high heat. Once the cooked pasta has stood in the colander for a while and is very dry, add ⅓ of the pasta to the hot oil, and fry for about 3 minutes, or until the edges are nice and crispy. Use a slotted spoon to transfer the crisped pasta to a paper towel-lined plate. Reserve the oil for serving.
3. Stir the remaining cooked pasta into the pot of soup.
4. Ladle the soup into bowls, and garnish with the crispy pasta, and a few drops of the reserved oil from the frying pan. Serve hot, and enjoy!

CHAPTER 7: VEGETABLES

ROASTED ARTICHOKES WITH LEMON VINAIGRETTE

INGREDIENTS FOR 4 SERVINGS:

- 3 lemons
- 4 artichokes (8 to 10 ounces each)
- 9 tbsp. extra-virgin olive oil
- Salt and pepper
- ½ tsp. garlic, minced to paste
- ½ tsp. Dijon mustard
- 2 tsp. chopped fresh parsley

DIRECTIONS:

1. Adjust oven rack to lower-middle position and heat oven to 475 degrees. Cut 1 lemon in half, squeeze halves into container filled with 2 quarts water, then add spent halves.
2. Working with 1 artichoke at a time, trim stem to about ¾ inch and cut of top quarter of artichoke. Break of bottom 3 or 4 rows of tough outer leaves by pulling them downward. Using paring knife, trim outer layer of stem and base, removing any dark green parts. Cut artichoke in half lengthwise, then remove fuzzy choke and any tiny inner purple-tinged leaves using small spoon. Submerge prepped artichokes in lemon water.
3. Coat bottom of 13 by 9-inch baking dish with 1 tbsp. oil. Remove artichokes from lemon water and shake of water, leaving some water still clinging to leaves. Toss artichokes with 2 tbsp. oil, ¾ tsp. salt, and pinch pepper; gently rub oil and seasonings between leaves. Arrange artichokes cut side down in prepared dish. Trim ends of remaining 2 lemons, halve crosswise, and arrange cut side up next to artichokes. Cover tightly with aluminum foil and roast until cut sides of artichokes begin to brown and bases and leaves are tender when poked with tip of paring knife, 25 to 30 minutes.
4. Transfer artichokes to serving platter. Let lemons cool slightly, then squeeze into fine-mesh strainer set over bowl, extracting as much juice and pulp as possible; press firmly on solids to yield 1½ tbsp. juice. Whisk garlic, mustard, and ½ tsp. salt into juice. Whisking constantly, slowly drizzle in remaining 6 tbsp. oil until emulsified. Whisk in parsley and season with salt and pepper to taste. Serve artichokes with dressing.

SAUTÉED SWISS CHARD WITH GARLIC

INGREDIENTS FOR 4 SERVINGS:

- 2 tbsp. extra-virgin olive oil
- 3 garlic cloves, sliced thin
- 1½ pounds Swiss chard, stems sliced ¼ inch thick on bias, leaves sliced into ½ -inch-wide strips
- Salt and pepper
- 2 tsp. lemon juice

DIRECTIONS:

1. Heat oil in 12-inch nonstick skillet over medium-high heat until just shimmering. Add garlic and cook, stirring constantly, until lightly browned, 30 to 60 seconds. Add chard stems and ⅛ tsp. salt and cook, stirring occasionally, until spotty brown and crisp-tender, about 6 minutes.
2. Add two-thirds of chard leaves and cook, tossing with tongs, until just starting to wilt, 30 to 60 seconds. Add remaining chard leaves and continue to cook, stirring frequently, until leaves are tender, about 3 minutes. Off heat, stir in lemon juice and season with salt and pepper to taste.

STUFFED BELL PEPPERS WITH SPICED BEEF, CURRANTS, AND FETA

 INGREDIENTS FOR 4 SERVINGS:

- 4 red, yellow, or orange bell peppers, ½ inch trimmed of tops, cores and
- seeds discarded
- Salt and pepper
- ½ cup long-grain white rice
- 1 tbsp. extra-virgin olive oil, plus extra for serving
- 1 onion, chopped ine
- 3 garlic cloves, minced
- 2 tsp. grated fresh ginger
- 2 tsp. ground cumin
- ¾ tsp. ground cardamom
- ½ tsp. red pepper lakes
- ¼ tsp. ground cinnamon
- 10 ounces 90 percent lean ground beef
- 1 (14.5-ounce) can diced tomatoes, drained with 2 tbsp. juice reserved
- ¼ cup currants
- 2 tsp. chopped fresh oregano or ½ tsp. dried
- 2 ounces feta cheese, crumbled (½ cup)
- ¼ cup slivered almonds, toasted and chopped

 DIRECTIONS:

1. Bring 4 quarts water to boil in large pot. Add bell peppers and 1 tbsp. salt and cook until just beginning to soften, 3 to 5 minutes. Using tongs, remove peppers from pot, drain excess water, and place peppers cut side up on paper towels. Return water to boil, add rice, and cook until tender, about 13 minutes. Drain rice and transfer to large bowl; set aside.
2. Adjust oven rack to middle position and heat oven to 350 degrees. Heat oil in 12-inch skillet over medium-high heat until shimmering. Add onion and ¼ tsp. salt and cook until softened and lightly browned, 5 to 7 minutes. Stir in garlic, ginger, cumin, cardamom, pepper flakes, and cinnamon and cook until fragrant, about 30 seconds. Add ground beef and cook, breaking up meat with wooden spoon, until no longer pink, about 4 minutes. Off heat, stir in tomatoes and reserved juice, currants, and oregano, scraping up any browned bits. Transfer mixture to bowl with rice. Add ¼ cup feta and almonds and gently toss to combine. Season with salt and pepper to taste.
3. Place peppers cut side up in 8-inch square baking dish. Pack each pepper with rice mixture, mounding filling on top. Bake until filling is heated through, about 30 minutes. Sprinkle remaining ¼ cup feta over peppers and drizzle with extra oil.

TAHINI SAUCE

 INGREDIENTS FOR 1¼ CUPS:

- ½ cup tahini
- ½ cup water
- ¼ cup lemon juice (2 lemons)

- 2 garlic cloves, minced
- Salt and pepper

DIRECTIONS:

1. Whisk tahini, water, lemon juice, and garlic together in bowl until combined. Season with salt and pepper to taste. Let sit until lavors meld, about 30 minutes. (Sauce can be refrigerated for up to 4 days.)

STUFFED EGGPLANT WITH BULGUR

INGREDIENTS FOR 4 SERVINGS:

- 4 (10-ounce) Italian eggplants, halved lengthwise
- 2 tbsp. extra-virgin olive oil
- Salt and pepper
- ½ cup medium-grind bulgur, rinsed
- ¼ cup water
- 1 onion, chopped ine
- 3 garlic cloves, minced
- 2 tsp. minced fresh oregano or ½ tsp. dried
- ¼ tsp. ground cinnamon
- Pinch cayenne pepper
- 1 pound plum tomatoes, cored, seeded, and chopped
- 2 ounces Pecorino Romano cheese, grated (1 cup)
- 2 tbsp. pine nuts, toasted
- 2 tsp. red wine vinegar
- 2 tbsp. minced fresh parsley

DIRECTIONS:

1. Adjust oven racks to upper-middle and lowest positions, place parchment paper–lined rimmed baking sheet on lowest rack, and heat oven to 400 degrees.
2. Score flesh of each eggplant half in 1-inch diamond pattern, about 1 inch deep. Brush scored sides of eggplant with 1 tbsp. oil and season with salt and pepper. Lay eggplant cut side down on hot sheet and roast until flesh is tender, 40 to 50 minutes. Transfer eggplant cut side down to paper towel–lined baking sheet and let drain.
3. Toss bulgur with water in bowl and let sit until grains are softened and liquid is fully absorbed, 20 to 40 minutes.
4. Heat remaining 1 tbsp. oil in 12-inch skillet over medium heat until shimmering. Add onion and cook until softened, 5 minutes. Stir in garlic, oregano, ½ tsp. salt, cinnamon, and cayenne and cook until fragrant, about 30 seconds. Off heat, stir in bulgur, tomatoes, ¾ cup Pecorino, pine nuts, and vinegar and let sit until heated through, about 1 minute. Season with salt and pepper to taste.
5. Return eggplant cut side up to rimmed baking sheet. Using 2 forks, gently push eggplant flesh to sides to make room for filling. Mound bulgur mixture into eggplant halves and pack lightly with back of spoon. Sprinkle with remaining ¼ cup Pecorino. Bake on upper rack until cheese is melted, 5 to 10 minutes. Sprinkle with parsley and serve.

SAUTÉED CABBAGE WITH PARSLEY AND LEMON

INGREDIENTS FOR 4 SERVINGS:

- 1 small head green cabbage (1¼ pounds), cored and sliced thin 2 tbsp. extra-virgin olive oil
- 1 onion, halved and sliced thin
- Salt and pepper
- ¼ cup chopped fresh parsley
- 1½ tsp. lemon juice

DIRECTIONS:

1. Place cabbage in large bowl and cover with cold water. Let sit for 3 minutes; drain well.
2. Heat 1 tbsp. oil in 12-inch nonstick skillet over medium-high heat until shimmering. Add onion and ¼ tsp. salt and cook until softened and lightly browned, 5 to 7 minutes; transfer to bowl.
3. Heat remaining 1 tbsp. oil in now-empty skillet over medium-high heat until shimmering. Add cabbage and sprinkle with ½ tsp. salt and ¼ tsp. pepper. Cover and cook, without stirring, until cabbage is wilted and lightly browned on bottom, about 3 minutes. Stir and continue to cook, uncovered, until cabbage is crisp-tender and lightly browned in places, about 4 minutes, stirring once halfway through cooking. Of heat, stir in onion, parsley, and lemon juice. Season with salt and pepper to taste and serve.

ROASTED MUSHROOMS WITH PARMESAN AND PINE NUTS

 INGREDIENTS FOR 4 SERVINGS:

- Salt and pepper
- 1½ pounds cremini mushrooms, trimmed and left whole if small, halved if medium, or quartered if large
- 1 pound shiitake mushrooms, stemmed, caps larger than
- 3 inches halved 3 tbsp. extra-virgin olive oil
- 1 tsp. lemon juice
- 1 ounce Parmesan cheese, grated (½ cup)
- 2 tbsp. pine nuts, toasted
- 2 tbsp. chopped fresh parsley

 DIRECTIONS:

1. Adjust oven rack to lowest position and heat oven to 450 degrees. Dissolve 5 tsp. salt in 2 quarts room-temperature water in large container. Add cremini mushrooms and shiitake mushrooms, cover with plate or bowl to submerge, and soak at room temperature for 10 minutes.
2. Drain mushrooms and pat dry with paper towels. Toss mushrooms with 2 tbsp. oil, then spread into single layer in rimmed baking sheet. Roast until liquid from mushrooms has completely evaporated, 35 to 45 minutes.
3. Remove sheet from oven (be careful of escaping steam when opening oven) and, using metal spatula, carefully stir mushrooms. Return to oven and continue to roast until mushrooms are deeply browned, 5 to 10 minutes.
4. Whisk remaining 1 tbsp. oil and lemon juice together in large bowl. Add mushrooms and toss to coat. Stir in Parmesan, pine nuts, and parsley and season with salt and pepper to taste. Serve immediately.

CUCUMBER-YOGURT SAUCE

 INGREDIENTS FOR ABOUT 2½ CUPS:

- 1 cup plain Greek yogurt
- 2 tbsp. extra-virgin olive oil
- 2 tbsp. minced fresh dill
- 1 garlic clove, minced
- 1 cucumber, peeled, halved lengthwise, seeded, and shredded Salt and pepper

 DIRECTIONS:

1. Whisk yogurt, oil, dill, and garlic together in medium bowl until combined. Stir in cucumber and season with salt and pepper to taste. (Sauce can be refrigerated for up to 1 day.)

ONE-POT CURRIED HALLOUMI

 INGREDIENTS FOR 4 SERVINGS:

- 2 tbsp. extra-virgin olive oil
- 2 packs halloumi cheese
- 1 cup water
- ½ cup coconut milk
- ¼ cup tomato paste
- ¼ tsp. white pepper
- ½ tsp. ground turmeric
- 1 ½ tsp. mild curry powder
- ½ tsp. garlic powder
- 1 tsp. onion powder
- 1 small cauliflower, cut into small florets
- Himalayan salt
- 2 tbsp. coconut flour
- Fresh coriander leaves, chopped, for serving
- Cooked rice for serving

DIRECTIONS:

1. In a large frying pan over medium-high heat, heat the olive oil. Chop the halloumi into 8 slices, about ¾-inch thick. When the oil is nice and hot, add the halloumi to the pan. You may work in batches if all of the cheese does not fit comfortably in the pan. Fry the halloumi on all sides until golden brown. Don't stress if the cheese is difficult to turn at first, it will become easier the crispier the outer coating becomes. Transfer to a platter, and keep warm.
2. In the same frying pan, stir in the water, coconut milk, tomato paste, pepper, turmeric, curry powder, garlic powder, and onion powder. When the sauce begins to boil, add the cauliflower florets, and season to taste with salt. Simmer the florets for 7-10 minutes with the lid on the pan, or until the cauliflower is fork-tender.
3. When the cauliflower is tender, add the coconut flour to the pan, and stir until the sauce thickens. Stir in the cooked halloumi until heated through.
4. Plate the curried halloumi with the sauce, along with rice of your choice. Garnish with the coriander leaves, and serve hot.

RICOTTA SALATA PASTA

 INGREDIENTS FOR 4 SERVINGS:

- 1 lb. fusilli
- ⅓ cup avocado oil
- ¼ tsp. white pepper
- ½ tsp. lemon zest, finely grated
- 1 tbsp. freshly squeezed lemon juice

- 3 tsp. crushed garlic
- 2 cups fresh mint leaves, chopped (more for garnish)
- ¼ cup almond slivers
- ½ cup ricotta Salata, grated (more for garnish)

DIRECTIONS:

1. Cook the fusilli in salted water, according to package instructions.
2. Meanwhile, pulse the avocado oil, pepper, zest, lemon juice, garlic, mint leaves, and almond slivers on high in a food processor, until you have a lump-free sauce. Add ½ cup of cheese, and pulse a few times until all of the ingredients are properly combined.
3. Once the pasta is cooked, drain through a colander set over the sink. Transfer to a serving bowl, and scrape the sauce from the food processor onto the cooked pasta. Gently stir to combine. Garnish with mint and extra cheese before serving hot.

GRILLED ZUCCHINI AND RED ONION WITH LEMON-BASIL DRESSING

 INGREDIENTS FOR 4 SERVINGS:

- 1 large red onion, peeled and sliced into ½-inch-thick rings 1 pound zucchini, sliced lengthwise into ¾-inch-thick planks 6 tbsp. extra-virgin olive oil
- Salt and pepper

- 1 tsp. grated lemon zest plus 1 tbsp. juice
- 1 small garlic clove, minced
- ¼ tsp. Dijon mustard
- 1 tbsp. chopped fresh basil

 DIRECTIONS:

1. 1. Thread onion rounds from side to side onto two 12-inch metal skewers. Brush onion and zucchini with ¼ cup oil, sprinkle with 1 tsp. salt, and season with pepper. Whisk remaining 2 tbsp. oil, lemon zest and juice, garlic, mustard, and ¼ tsp. salt together in bowl; set aside for serving.
2. 2a. FOR A CHARCOAL GRILL Open bottom vent completely. Light large chimney starter half filled with charcoal briquettes (3 quarts). When top coals are partially covered with ash, pour evenly over grill. Set cooking grate in place, cover, and open lid vent completely. Heat grill until hot, about 5 minutes.
3. 2b. FOR A GAS GRILL Turn all burners to high, cover, and heat grill until hot, about 15 minutes. Turn all burners to medium.
4. Clean and oil cooking grate. Place vegetables cut side down on grill. Cook (covered if using gas), turning as needed, until tender and caramelized, 18 to 22 minutes; transfer vegetables to serving platter as they finish cooking. Remove skewers from onion and discard any charred outer rings. Whisk dressing to recombine, then drizzle over vegetables. Sprinkle with basil and serve.

CROATIAN DOUBLE-CRUSTED VEGETABLE TART

 INGREDIENTS FOR 4 SERVINGS:

- 1 ¼ tsp. Himalayan salt
- 4 ½ cups all-purpose flour
- 1 cup warm water
- 1 ½ cups avocado oil (plus 3 tbsp.)

- ¼ small green cabbage, thinly sliced
- 1 lb. spinach, ribs removed, and leaves chopped
- ¼ tsp. white pepper
- 4 tsp. crushed garlic

DIRECTIONS:

1. Place 1 tsp. of salt, along with the 4 ½ cups of flour, in a medium-sized bowl, and whisk to combine. Pour the warm water and 1 ½ cups of oil into the bowl, and stir with a fork, until the mixture just comes together. Use your hands to bring the dough together in a ball. Cover in cling wrap, and chill for 30 minutes.
2. Meanwhile, place the cabbage and spinach in a clean mixing bowl, and add 2 tbsp. of oil, and the remaining salt and pepper. Toss until all of the vegetables are evenly coated.
3. Set the oven to preheat to 400°F, with the wire rack in the center of the oven.
4. When the dough is nicely chilled. Divide into two balls, and place the balls on two pieces of lightly floured greaseproof paper. Roll the balls into ¼-inch thick circles.
5. Spread the coated vegetables over one of the dough circles, leaving a small border around the edges. Carefully place the second round over the vegetables to create a lid. Use a fork to seal the edges like a pie. Place the double-crusted tart on a lightly sprayed baking tray, and bake in the oven for 20 minutes, or until the crust is lightly browned.
6. While the tart is baking, place 1 tbsp. of oil with the crushed garlic in a small glass bowl, and whisk to combine.
7. When the tart is done, immediately brush the top crust with the oil and garlic. Slice, and serve while still hot.

MECHOUIA

DRESSING
- 2 tsp. coriander seeds
- 1½ tsp. caraway seeds
- 1 tsp. cumin seeds
- 5 tbsp. extra-virgin olive oil
- ½ tsp. paprika
- ⅛ tsp. cayenne pepper
- 3 garlic cloves, minced
- ¼ cup chopped fresh parsley
- ¼ cup chopped fresh cilantro
- 2 tbsp. chopped fresh mint

- 1 tsp. grated lemon zest plus 2 tbsp. juice
- Salt

VEGETABLES
- 2 red or green bell peppers, tops and bottoms trimmed, stemmed and seeded, and peppers lattened
- 1 small eggplant, halved lengthwise and scored on cut side
- 1 zucchini (8 to 10 ounces), halved lengthwise and scored on cut side 4 plum tomatoes, cored and halved lengthwise
- Salt and pepper
- 2 shallots, unpeeled

DIRECTIONS:

1. FOR THE DRESSING Grind coriander seeds, caraway seeds, and cumin seeds in spice grinder until finely ground. Whisk ground spices, oil, paprika, and cayenne together in bowl. Reserve 3 tbsp. oil mixture for brushing vegetables before grilling. Heat remaining oil mixture and garlic in 8-inch skillet over low heat, stirring occasionally, until fragrant and small bubbles appear, 8 to 10 minutes. Transfer to large bowl, let cool for 10 minutes, then whisk in parsley, cilantro, mint, and lemon zest and juice and season with salt to taste; set aside for serving.
2. FOR THE VEGETABLES Brush interior of bell peppers and cut sides of eggplant, zucchini, and tomatoes with reserved oil mixture and season with salt.
3. 3a. FOR A CHARCOAL GRILL Open bottom vent completely. Light large chimney starter three-quarters filled with charcoal briquettes (4½ quarts). When top coals are partially covered with ash, pour evenly over grill. Set cooking grate in place, cover, and open lid vent completely. Heat grill until hot, about 5 minutes.
4. 3b. FOR A GAS GRILL Turn all burners to high, cover, and heat grill until hot, about 15 minutes. Turn all burners to medium-high.
5. Clean and oil cooking grate. Place bell peppers, eggplant, zucchini, tomatoes, and shallots cut side down on grill. Cook (covered if using gas), turning as needed, until tender and slightly charred, 8 to 16 minutes. Transfer eggplant, zucchini, tomatoes, and shallots to baking sheet as they finish cooking; place bell peppers in bowl, cover with plastic wrap, and let steam to loosen skins.
6. Let vegetables cool slightly. Peel bell peppers, tomatoes, and shallots. Chop all vegetables into ½-inch pieces, then toss gently with dressing in bowl. Season with salt and pepper to taste. Serve warmor at room temperature.

BRAISED CAULIFLOWER WITH GARLIC AND WHITE WINE

INGREDIENTS FOR 4 SERVINGS:

- 3 tbsp. plus 1 tsp. extra-virgin olive oil
- 3 garlic cloves, minced
- ⅛ tsp. red pepper lakes
- 1 head cauliower (2 pounds), cored and cut into 1½-inch lorets Salt and pepper

- ⅓ cup chicken or vegetable broth
- ⅓ cup dry white wine
- 2 tbsp. minced fresh parsley

DIRECTIONS:

1. Combine 1 tsp. oil, garlic, and pepper flakes in small bowl. Heat remaining 3 tbsp. oil in 12-inch skillet over medium-high heat until shimmering. Add cauliflower and ¼ tsp. salt and cook, stirring occasionally, until florets are golden brown, 7 to 9 minutes.
2. Push cauliflower to sides of skillet. Add garlic mixture to center and cook, mashing mixture into skillet, until fragrant, about 30 seconds. Stir garlic mixture into cauliflower.
3. Stir in broth and wine and bring to simmer. Reduce heat to medium-low, cover, and cook until cauliflower is crisp-tender, 4 to 6 minutes. Of heat, stir in parsley and season with salt and pepper to taste.

STUFFED EGGPLANTS

 INGREDIENTS FOR 4 SERVINGS:

- 2 large eggplants
- 1 shallot, chopped
- 4 garlic cloves, minced
- 2 tbsp. olive oil
- 2 chicken sausages

- ¼ cup chopped parsley
- 1 tsp. balsamic vinegar
- ½ cup grated Parmesan
- Salt and pepper to taste

 DIRECTIONS:

1. Cut the eggplants in half and remove the flesh. Chop it finely. Reserve the casings of the eggplants intact.
2. Remove the casings from the chicken sausages and shred the meat.
3. Heat the oil in a skillet and stir in the sausage. Cook for 5 minutes then add the shallot and garlic, as well as the eggplants.
4. Cook for another 5 minutes then remove from heat. Add the parsley and vinegar.
5. Place the casings in a deep dish baking pan.
6. Fill the skins with the cooked mixture and top with grated cheese.
7. Cook in the preheated oven at 350F for 20 minutes.
8. Serve the eggplants warm and fresh.

ROASTED CELERY ROOT WITH YOGURT AND SESAME SEEDS

 **INGREDIENTS FOR 6 SERVINGS:**

- 3 celery roots (2½ pounds), peeled, halved, and sliced ½ inch thick 3 tbsp. extra-virgin olive oil
- Salt and pepper
- ¼ cup plain yogurt
- ¼ tsp. grated lemon zest plus 1 tsp. juice

- 1 tsp. sesame seeds, toasted
- 1 tsp. coriander seeds, toasted and crushed
- ¼ tsp. dried thyme
- ¼ cup fresh cilantro leaves

DIRECTIONS:

1. Adjust oven rack to lowest position and heat oven to 425 degrees. Toss celery root with oil, ½ tsp. salt, and ¼ tsp. pepper and arrange in rimmed baking sheet in single layer. Roast celery root until sides touching sheet toward back of oven are well browned, 25 to 30 minutes. Rotate sheet and continue to roast until sides touching sheet toward back of oven are well browned, 6 to 10 minutes.
2. Use metal spatula to flip each piece and continue to roast until celery root is very tender and sides touching sheet are browned, 10 to 15 minutes.
   Transfer celery root to serving platter. Whisk yogurt, lemon zest and juice, and pinch salt together in bowl. In separate bowl, combine sesame seeds, coriander seeds, thyme, and pinch salt. Drizzle celery root with yogurt sauce and sprinkle with seed mixture and cilantro.

GREEK-STYLE GARLIC-LEMON POTATOES

 INGREDIENTS FOR 4 SERVINGS:

- 3 tbsp. extra-virgin olive oil
- 1½ pounds Yukon Gold potatoes, peeled and cut lengthwise into ¾-inch- thick wedges
- 1½ tbsp. minced fresh oregano

- 3 garlic cloves, minced
- 2 tsp. grated lemon zest plus 1½ tbsp. juice
- Salt and pepper
- 1½ tbsp. minced fresh parsley

DIRECTIONS:

1. Heat 2 tbsp. oil in 12-inch nonstick skillet over medium-high heat until shimmering. Add potatoes cut side down in single layer and cook until golden brown on first side (skillet should sizzle but not smoke), about 6 minutes. Using tongs, flip potatoes onto second cut side and cook until golden brown, about 5 minutes. Reduce heat to medium-low, cover, and cook until potatoes are tender, 8 to 12 minutes.
2. Meanwhile, whisk remaining 1 tbsp. oil, oregano, garlic, lemon zest and juice, ½ tsp. salt, and ½ tsp. pepper together in small bowl. When potatoes are tender, gently stir in garlic mixture and cook, uncovered, until fragrant, about 2 minutes. Of heat, gently stir in parsley and season with salt and pepper to taste.

CHAPTER 8: SALAD

BASIC GREEN SALAD

 INGREDIENTS FOR 4 SERVINGS:

- ½ garlic clove, peeled
- 8 ounces (8 cups) lettuce, torn into bite-size pieces if necessary Extra-virgin olive oil
- Vinegar
- Salt and pepper

DIRECTIONS:

1. Rub inside of salad bowl with garlic. Add lettuce. Holding thumb over mouth of olive oil bottle to control low, slowly drizzle lettuce with small amount of oil. Toss greens very gently. Continue to drizzle with oil and toss gently until greens are lightly coated and just glistening. Sprinkle with small amounts of vinegar, salt, and pepper to taste and toss gently to coat.

TAHINI-LEMON DRESSING

 INGREDIENTS FOR ABOUT ½ CUP:

- 2½ tbsp. lemon juice
- 2 tbsp. tahini
- 1 tbsp. water
- 1 garlic clove, minced
- ½ tsp. salt
- ⅛ tsp. pepper
- ¼ cup extra-virgin olive oil

DIRECTIONS:

1. Whisk lemon juice, tahini, water, garlic, salt, and pepper together in bowl until smooth.
2. Whisking constantly, slowly drizzle in oil until emulsiied. (Dressing can be refrigerated for up to 1 week.)

BITTER GREENS SALAD WITH OLIVES AND FETA

 INGREDIENTS FOR 4 SERVINGS:

- 1 head escarole (1 pound), trimmed and cut into 1-inch pieces
- 1 small head frisée (4 ounces), trimmed and torn into 1-inch pieces ½ cup pitted kalamata olives, halved
- 2 ounces feta cheese, crumbled (½ cup)
- ⅓ cup pepperoncini, seeded and cut into ¼-inch-thick strips
- ⅓ cup chopped fresh dill
- 2 tbsp. lemon juice
- 1 garlic clove, minced
- Salt and pepper
- 3 tbsp. extra-virgin olive oil

 DIRECTIONS:

1. Gently toss escarole, frisée, olives, feta, and pepperoncini together in large bowl. Whisk dill, lemon juice, garlic, ¼ tsp. salt, and ⅛ tsp. pepper together in small bowl. Whisking constantly, slowly drizzle in oil. Drizzle dressing over salad and gently toss to coat.

ASPARAGUS SALAD WITH ORANGES, FETA, AND HAZELNUTS

 INGREDIENTS FOR 6 SERVINGS:

PESTO
- 2 cups fresh mint leaves
- ¼ cup fresh basil leaves
- ¼ cup grated Pecorino Romano cheese
- 1 tsp. grated lemon zest plus 2 tsp. juice
- 1 garlic clove, minced
- Salt and pepper
- ½ cup extra-virgin olive oil

SALAD
- 2 pounds asparagus, trimmed
- 2 oranges
- 4 ounces feta cheese, crumbled (1 cup)
- ¾ cup hazelnuts, toasted, skinned, and chopped
- Salt and pepper

 DIRECTIONS:

1. FOR THE PESTO Process mint, basil, Pecorino, lemon zest and juice, garlic, and ¾ tsp. salt in food processor until finely chopped, about 20 seconds, scraping down sides of bowl as needed. Transfer to large bowl. Stir in oil and season with salt and pepper to taste.
2. FOR THE SALAD Cut asparagus tips from stalks into ¾-inch-long pieces. Slice asparagus stalks ⅛ inch thick on bias into approximate 2-inch lengths. Cut away peel and pith from oranges. Holding fruit over bowl, use paring knife to slice between membranes to release segments. Add asparagus tips and stalks, orange segments, feta, and hazelnuts to pesto and toss to combine. Season with salt and pepper to taste.

MOROCCAN-STYLE CARROT SALAD

 INGREDIENTS FOR 6 SERVINGS:

- 2 oranges
- 1 tbsp. lemon juice
- 1 tsp. honey
- ¾ tsp. ground cumin
- ⅛ tsp. cayenne pepper
- ⅛ tsp. ground cinnamon
  Salt and pepper
- 1 pound carrots, peeled and shredded
- 3 tbsp. minced fresh cilantro
- 3 tbsp. extra-virgin olive oil

 DIRECTIONS:

1. Cut away peel and pith from oranges. Holding fruit over bowl, use paring knife to slice between membranes to release segments. Cut segments in half crosswise and let drain in fine-mesh strainer set over large bowl, reserving juice.
2. Whisk lemon juice, honey, cumin, cayenne, cinnamon, and ½ tsp. salt into reserved orange juice. Add drained oranges and carrots and gently toss to coat. Let sit until liquid starts to pool in bottom of bowl, 3 to 5 minutes.
3. Drain salad in fine-mesh strainer and return to now-empty bowl. Stir in cilantro and oil and season with salt and pepper to taste.

FENNEL AND APPLE SALAD WITH SMOKED MACKEREL

 INGREDIENTS FOR 6 SERVINGS:

- 3 tbsp. lemon juice
- 1 tbsp. whole-grain mustard
- 1 small shallot, minced
- 2 tsp. minced fresh tarragon
- Salt and pepper
- ¼ cup extra-virgin olive oil
- 5 ounces (5 cups) watercress
- 2 Granny Smith apples, peeled, cored, and cut into 3-inch-long matchsticks 1 fennel bulb, stalks discarded, bulb halved, cored, and sliced thin
- 6 ounces smoked mackerel, skin and pin bones removed, laked

 DIRECTIONS:

1. Whisk lemon juice, mustard, shallot, 1 tsp. tarragon, ½ tsp. salt, and ¼ tsp. pepper together in large bowl. Whisking constantly, slowly drizzle in oil. Add watercress, apples, and fennel and gently toss to coat. Season with salt and pepper to taste.
2. Divide salad among plates and top with flaked mackerel. Drizzle any remaining dressing over mackerel and sprinkle with remaining 1 tsp. tarragon. Serve immediately.

ROASTED WINTER SQUASH SALAD WITH ZA'ATAR AND PARSLEY

 INGREDIENTS FOR 6 SERVINGS:

- 3 pounds butternut squash, peeled, seeded, and cut into ½-inch pieces (8 cups)
- ¼ cup extra-virgin olive oil
- Salt and pepper
- 1 tsp. za'atar
- 1 small shallot, minced

- 2 tbsp. lemon juice
- 2 tbsp. honey
- ¾ cup fresh parsley leaves
- ⅓ cup roasted, unsalted pepitas
- ½ cup pomegranate seeds

 DIRECTIONS:

1. Adjust oven rack to lowest position and heat oven to 450 degrees. Toss squash with 1 tbsp. oil and season with salt and pepper. Arrange squash in single layer in rimmed baking sheet and roast until well browned and tender, 30 to 35 minutes, stirring halfway through roasting. Sprinkle squash with za'atar and let cool for 15 minutes.
2. Whisk shallot, lemon juice, honey, and ¼ tsp. salt together in large bowl. Whisking constantly, slowly drizzle in remaining 3 tbsp. oil. Add squash, parsley, and pepitas and gently toss to coat. Arrange salad on serving platter and sprinkle with pomegranate seeds.

MEDITERRANEAN-STYLE TUNA SALAD

 INGREDIENTS FOR 4 SERVINGS:

- 1 tsp. Himalayan salt
- 3 tbsp. white wine vinegar
- ¼ cup extra-virgin olive oil
- 1 tsp. crushed garlic

- 1 medium red bell pepper, seeded and diced
- 1 cup pitted green olives
- 6 oz. canned tuna in olive oil, well-drained
- 1 bag mixed salad greens

 DIRECTIONS:

1. Place the salt, vinegar, and oil in a large mixing bowl. Whisk until properly combined.
2. Gently stir in the garlic, bell peppers, and olives. Add the drained tuna, and stir until all of the ingredients are properly combined. Seal the bowl, and chill for a minimum of 1 hour.
3. Serve the chilled tuna mixture on a bed of mixed salad greens.

FRESH MINT & TOASTED PITA SALAD

 INGREDIENTS FOR 4 SERVINGS:

- ¼ tsp. freshly ground black pepper
- ½ tsp. ground sumac (extra for garnish)
- 1 tsp. Himalayan salt
- 1 tsp. crushed garlic
- ½ cup extra-virgin olive oil
- ½ cup freshly squeezed lemon juice
- 2 whole-wheat pita bread rounds, toasted, and broken into bite-sized pieces

- 1 bunch spring onions, thinly sliced
- 1 small green bell pepper, diced
- ¼ cup fresh mint leaves, chopped
- ½ cup fresh parsley, chopped
- 2 heirloom tomatoes, diced
- 2 small English cucumbers, diced
- 2 cups romaine lettuce, shredded

DIRECTIONS:

1. In a small glass bowl, whisk together the pepper, sumac, salt, garlic, olive oil, and lemon juice. Set aside.
2. In a large mixing bowl, toss together the toasted pita bites, spring onions, bell pepper, mint, parsley, tomatoes, cucumbers, and shredded lettuce. Drizzle the with the olive oil dressing, and serve immediately, garnished with the extra ground sumac.

LEMON & MINT-TOPPED GARDEN SALAD

😋 INGREDIENTS FOR 4 SERVINGS:

- ⅛ tsp. Himalayan salt (extra if needed)
- 1 tsp. fresh mint, chopped
- 2 tbsp. extra-virgin olive oil
- 1 small lemon, juiced
- ½ medium English cucumber, thinly sliced
- 1 heirloom tomato, roughly chopped
- 4-5 cups mixed salad greens, shredded
- White pepper

😋 DIRECTIONS:

1. In a small glass bowl, whisk together the salt, mint, olive oil, and lemon juice. Set aside.
2. Place the cucumber, tomato, and salad greens in a bowl. Season to taste with extra salt and pepper, if desired, and toss to combine. Drizzle with the lemon and mint mixture before serving.
3. Tip: Any extra lemon mixture may be refrigerated, and reserved for other dishes.

GRILLED CHICKEN SALAD

😋 INGREDIENTS FOR 4 SERVINGS:

- 2 chicken fillets
- 1 tsp. dried oregano
- 1 tsp. dried basil
- 2 tbsp. olive oil
- 2 cups arugula leaves
- 1 cup cherry tomatoes, halved
- ¼ cup green olives
- 1 cucumber, sliced
- 1 lemon, juiced
- 2 tbsp. extra virgin olive oil
- Salt and pepper to taste

😋 DIRECTIONS:

1. Season the chicken with salt, pepper, oregano and basil then drizzle it with olive oil.
2. Heat a grill pan over medium flame then place the chicken on the grill. Cook on each side until browned then cut into thin strips.
3. Combine the chicken with the rest of the ingredients and mix gently.
4. Adjust the taste with salt and pepper and serve the salad as fresh as possible.

ROASTED BELL PEPPER SALAD WITH ANCHOVY DRESSING

😋 INGREDIENTS FOR 4 SERVINGS:

- 8 roasted red bell peppers, sliced
- 2 tbsp. pine nuts
- 1 cup cherry tomatoes, halved
- 2 tbsp. chopped parsley
- 4 anchovy fillets
- 1 lemon, juiced
- 1 garlic clove
- 1 tbsp. extra-virgin olive oil
- Salt and pepper to taste

😋 DIRECTIONS:

1. Combine the anchovy fillets, lemon juice, garlic and olive oil in a mortar and mix them well.
2. Mix the rest of the ingredients in a salad bowl then drizzle in the dressing.
3. Serve the salad as fresh as possible.

PITA BREAD BEAN SALAD

👥 INGREDIENTS FOR 4 SERVINGS:

- 1 can red beans, drained
- 1 red onion, sliced
- 2 tomatoes, cubed
- 2 pita breads, cubed

- 2 tbsp. extra virgin olive oil
- 1 tbsp. balsamic vinegar
- Salt and pepper to taste

✗ DIRECTIONS:

1. Combine the beans, red onion, pita bread, oil and vinegar in a salad bowl.
2. Season with salt and pepper and serve the salad as fresh as possible.

ROASTED BROCCOLI SALAD

👥 INGREDIENTS FOR 4 SERVINGS:

- 2 pounds broccoli, cut into florets
- 2 garlic cloves, chopped
- 2 tbsp. extra virgin olive oil
- 1 red pepper, chopped

- 1 cup cherry tomatoes, halved
- 1 tsp. capers, chopped
- ¼ cup green olives, sliced
- Salt and pepper to taste

✗ DIRECTIONS:

1. Combine the broccoli, garlic, oil, salt and pepper in a deep dish baking pan.
2. Cook in the preheated oven at 350F for 10 minutes.
3. Transfer the broccoli in a salad bowl then add the rest of the ingredients.
4. Season with salt and pepper and serve the salad fresh.

WARM SHRIMP AND ARUGULA SALAD

👥 INGREDIENTS FOR 4 SERVINGS:

- 2 tbsp. extra virgin olive oil
- 2 garlic cloves, minced
- 1 red pepper, sliced
- 1 pound fresh shrimps, peeled and deveined

- 1 orange, juiced
- Salt and pepper to taste
- 3 cups arugula

✗ DIRECTIONS:

1. Heat the oil in a frying pan and stir in the garlic and red pepper. Cook for 1 minute then add the shrimps.
2. Cook for 5 minutes then add the orange juice and cook for another 5 more minutes.
3. When done, spoon the shrimps and the sauce over the arugula. 4. Serve the salad fresh.

RED BEET SPINACH SALAD

👥 INGREDIENTS FOR 4 SERVINGS:

- 3 cups baby spinach
- 2 red beets, cooked and diced
- 1 tbsp. prepared horseradish

- 1 tbsp. apple cider vinegar
- ¼ cup Greek yogurt
- Salt and pepper to taste

✗ DIRECTIONS:

1. Combine the baby spinach and red beets in a salad bowl.
2. Add the horseradish, vinegar and yogurt and mix well then season with salt and pepper.
3. Serve the salad as fresh as possible.

SMOKY EGGPLANT BALSAMIC SALAD

👥 INGREDIENTS FOR 4 SERVINGS:

- 2 eggplants, sliced
- 2 tbsp. extra virgin olive oil
- 2 garlic cloves, minced
- Salt and pepper to taste
- 1 tsp. smoked paprika
- 2 tbsp. sherry vinegar
- 2 cups mixed greens

🍴 DIRECTIONS:

1. Season the eggplant slices with salt and pepper.
2. Mix the oil with garlic and paprika then brush this mixture over the eggplant slices.
3. Heat a grill pan over medium flame then place the eggplant on the grill. Cook on each side until browned then transfer the vegetable in a salad bowl.
4. Add the sherry vinegar and greens and serve the salad fresh.

GRILLED SALMON BULGUR SALAD

👥 INGREDIENTS FOR 4 SERVINGS:

- 2 salmon fillets
- Salt and pepper to taste
- ½ cup bulgur
- 2 cups vegetable stock
- 1 cup cherry tomatoes, halved
- 1 cucumber, cubed
- 1 green onion, chopped
- ½ cup green olives, sliced
- 1 red bell pepper, cored and diced
- 1 red pepper, chopped
- ½ cup sweet corn
- 1 lemon, juiced

🍴 DIRECTIONS:

1. Season the salmon with salt and pepper and place it on a hot grill pan. Cook it on each side until browned.
2. Combine the bulgur and stock in a saucepan. Cook until all the liquid has been absorbed then transfer in a salad bowl.
3. Add the rest of the ingredients, including the salmon and season with salt and pepper.
4. Serve the salad fresh.

YOGURT ROMAINE SALAD

👥 INGREDIENTS FOR 4 SERVINGS:

- 1 head romaine lettuce, shredded
- 2 cucumbers, sliced
- ½ cup Greek yogurt
- 1 tsp. Dijon mustard
- 1 pinch chili powder
- 1 tbsp. lemon juice
- 2 tbsp. chopped dill
- 4 mint leaves, chopped
- 2 tbsp. extra virgin olive oil
- 2 garlic cloves, minced
- Salt and pepper to taste

🍴 DIRECTIONS:

1. Combine the lettuce with the cucumbers in a salad bowl.
2. For the dressing, mix the yogurt, mustard, chili, lemon juice, dill, mint, oil and garlic in a mortar. Add salt and pepper and mix well into a paste.
3. Drizzle the dressing over the salad and serve it fresh.

BEET TABBOULEH

 INGREDIENTS FOR 4 SERVINGS:

- ½ cup couscous
- 1 cup vegetable stock, hot
- 2 red beets, cooked and diced
- 2 tomatoes, diced
- 1 cup chopped parsley
- ¼ cup chopped cilantro
- 1 tbsp. chopped mint
- 2 tbsp. chopped chives
- 2 tbsp. pine nuts
- Salt and pepper to taste
- 1 lemon, juiced
- 4 oz. feta cheese, crumbled

DIRECTIONS:

1. Combine the couscous and hot stock in a bowland allow to soak up all the liquid.
2. Add the beets, tomatoes, parsley, cilantro, mint, chives and pine nuts.
3. Add salt and pepper to taste then drizzle in the lemon juice.
4. Top the salad with feta cheese and serve right away.

MEDITERRANEAN POTATO SALAD

 INGREDIENTS FOR 6 SERVINGS:

- 2 pounds new potatoes
- ¼ cup chopped parsley
- 2 tbsp. chopped dill
- 1 pinch chili flakes
- 1 lemon, juiced
- 1 tbsp. Dijon mustard
- 2 tbsp. extra virgin olive oil
- 1 tsp. red wine vinegar
- Salt and pepper to taste

DIRECTIONS:

1. Place the potatoes in a large pot and cover them with water. Add salt to taste and cook until tender. Drain well then cut into small cubes and place in a salad bowl.
2. Add the parsley, dill and chili flakes.
3. For the dressing, mix the lemon juice, mustard, oil and vinegar in a bowl. Add salt and pepper to taste and mix well.
4. Drizzle the dressing over the potatoes and mix well.
5. Serve the salad fresh.

ARUGULA SALAD WITH FENNEL AND SHAVED PARMESAN

INGREDIENTS FOR 6 SERVINGS:

- 6 ounces (6 cups) baby arugula
- 1 large fennel bulb, stalks discarded, bulb halved, cored, and sliced thin 1½ tbsp. lemon juice
- 1 small shallot, minced
- 1 tsp. Dijon mustard
- 1 tsp. minced fresh thyme
- 1 small garlic clove, minced
- Salt and pepper
- ¼ cup extra-virgin olive oil
- 1 ounce Parmesan cheese, shaved

DIRECTIONS:

1. Gently toss arugula and fennel together in large bowl. Whisk lemon juice, shallot, mustard, thyme, garlic, ⅛ tsp. salt, and pinch pepper together in small bowl. Whisking constantly, slowly drizzle in oil. Drizzle dressing over salad and gently toss to coat. Season with salt and pepper to taste. Serve, topping individual portions with Parmesan.

HERB VINAIGRETTE

INGREDIENTS FOR ABOUT ¼ CUPS:

- 1 tbsp. wine vinegar
- 1 tbsp. minced fresh parsley or chives
- 1½ tsp. minced shallot
- ½ tsp. minced fresh thyme, tarragon, marjoram, or oregano ½ tsp. mayonnaise
- ½ tsp. Dijon mustard
- ⅛ tsp. salt
- Pinch pepper
- 3 tbsp. extra-virgin olive oil

DIRECTIONS:

1. Whisk vinegar, parsley, shallot, thyme, mayonnaise, mustard, salt, and pepper together in bowl until smooth. Whisking constantly, slowly drizzle in oil until emulsiied.

MEDITERRANEAN QUINOA SALAD

INGREDIENTS FOR 4 SERVINGS:

- 1 ½ cups dry quinoa
- 1 pack salad savors
- ½ tsp. kosher salt
- 15 oz. garbanzo beans
- ½ cup extra virgin olive oil
- 3 cups arugula
- 1 tbsp. balsamic vinegar
- Black pepper, ground
- 2 cloves garlic, crushed
- ½ tsp. dried thyme
- ½ tsp. dry basil

INSTRUCTIONS:

1. Cook the quinoa in salted water till it turns soft according to the instructions on the packet.
2. In a small bowl, combine the olive oil, vinegar, basil, garlic, and thyme. Mix the ingredients to blend them well. Sprinkle some pepper and salt onto it to season it.
3. Combine the arugula, garbanzo beans, quinoa, and salad savors in a large bowl. Pour the dressing onto the contents and toss them around for a few seconds to coat it completely in the dressing.
4. Season it with salt and pepper if required and serve warm!

ARUGULA SALAD WITH PEAR, ALMONDS, GOAT CHEESE, AND APRICOTS

INGREDIENTS FOR 6 SERVINGS:

- 3 tbsp. white wine vinegar
- 1 tbsp. apricot jam (Honey can be substituted for the apricot jam)
- 1 small shallot, minced
- Salt and pepper
- ½ cup dried apricots, chopped
- 3 tbsp. extra-virgin olive oil
- ¼ small red onion, sliced thin
- 8 ounces (8 cups) baby arugula
- 1 ripe but irm pear, halved, cored, and sliced ¼ inch thick
- ⅓ cup sliced almonds, toasted
- 3 ounces goat cheese, crumbled (¾ cup)

DIRECTIONS:

1. Whisk vinegar, jam, shallot, ¼ tsp. salt, and ⅛ tsp. pepper together in large bowl. Add apricots, cover, and microwave until steaming, about 1 minute. Whisking constantly, slowly drizzle in oil. Stir in onion and let sit until figs are softened and vinaigrette has cooled to room temperature, about 15 minutes.
Just before serving, whisk vinaigrette to re-emulsify. Add arugula and pear and gently toss to coat. Season with salt and pepper to taste. Serve, topping individual portions with almonds and goat cheese.

BRIE ARUGULA SALAD

 INGREDIENTS FOR 4 SERVINGS:

- 2 cups arugula leaves
- 8 quail eggs, cooked and halved
- 8 oz. Brie cheese, crumbled
- 2 tbsp. balsamic vinegar
- 2 tbsp. extra virgin olive oil

DIRECTIONS:

1. Combine the arugula leaves, eggs, cheese, vinegar and oil in a salad bowl.
2. Mix gently and serve the salad fresh.

NICOISE SALAD

 INGREDIENTS FOR 4 SERVINGS:

- 4 eggs
- ¼ cup flat-leafed parsley, chopped
- ½ cup chopped potatoes
- 12 Nicoise olives
- ½ cup green beans halved
- 6 anchovy fillets, halved
- 2 tbsp. red wine vinegar
- 2 baby lettuces, leaves separated
- 1 tsp. Dijon mustard
- ½ cup extra virgin olive oil
- 2 garlic cloves, chopped
- 1 tsp. caster sugar

INSTRUCTIONS:

1. Boil the eggs in a pot of water for about 5 minutes. Remove them from the hot water and place them in a bowl of cold water immediately.
2. Boil the potatoes in a pot of salted water and then allow them to simmer for about 10 minutes to make them tender. Toss the beans in and allow them to simmer for 2 minutes before turning off the heat and placing the beans in cold water.
3. Chop the potatoes into halves or quarters if they are too big.
4. In a small bowl, combine the vinegar, garlic, sugar, mustard, pepper, and sea salt. Whisk the mixture well, and then slowly add in the olive oil. Keep whisking the mixture till it becomes a thick, smooth paste.
5. Combine the egg and lettuce in a bowl and then add in the potatoes, anchovies, beans, and olives. Top the entire dish with parsley.
6. Drizzle the dressing over the salad to serve.

GREEN SALAD WITH MARCONA ALMONDS AND MANCHEGO CHEESE

 INGREDIENTS FOR 4 SERVINGS:

- 6 ounces (6 cups) mesclun greens
- 5 tsp. sherry vinegar
- 1 shallot, minced
- 1 tsp. Dijon mustard
- Salt and pepper
- ¼ cup extra-virgin olive oil
- ⅓ cup Marcona almonds, chopped coarse
- 2 ounces Manchego cheese, shaved

DIRECTIONS:

1. Place mesclun in large bowl. Whisk vinegar, shallot, mustard, ¼ tsp. salt, and ¼ tsp. pepper together in small bowl. Whisking constantly, slowly drizzle in oil. Drizzle vinaigrette over mesclun and gently toss to coat. Season with salt and pepper to taste. Serve, topping individual portions with almonds and Manchego.

MÂCHE SALAD WITH CUCUMBER AND MINT

INGREDIENTS FOR 6 SERVINGS:

- 12 ounces (12 cups) mâche
- 1 cucumber, sliced thin
- ½ cup chopped fresh mint
- ⅓ cup pine nuts, toasted
- 1 tbsp. lemon juice
- 1 tbsp. minced fresh parsley
- 1 tbsp. capers, rinsed and minced
- 1 tsp. minced fresh thyme
- 1 garlic clove, minced
- Salt and pepper
- ¼ cup extra-virgin olive oil

DIRECTIONS:

1. Gently toss mâche, cucumber, mint, and pine nuts together in large bowl. Whisk lemon juice, parsley, capers, thyme, garlic, ¼ tsp. salt, and ¼ tsp. pepper together in small bowl. Whisking constantly, slowly drizzle in oil. Drizzle dressing over salad and gently toss to coat. Season with salt and pepper to taste.

MEDITERRANEAN CHOPPED SALAD

INGREDIENTS FOR 4 SERVINGS:

- 1 cucumber, peeled, halved lengthwise, seeded, and cut into ½-inch pieces
- 10 ounces grape tomatoes, quartered
- Salt and pepper
- 3 tbsp. red wine vinegar
- 1 garlic clove, minced
- 3 tbsp. extra-virgin olive oil
- 1 (15-ounce) can chickpeas, rinsed
- ½ cup pitted kalamata olives, chopped
- ½ small red onion, chopped ine
- ½ cup chopped fresh parsley
- 1 romaine lettuce heart (6 ounces), cut into ½-inch pieces
- 4 ounces feta cheese, crumbled (1 cup)

DIRECTIONS:

1. Toss cucumber and tomatoes with 1 tsp. salt and let drain in colander for 15 minutes.
2. Whisk vinegar and garlic together in large bowl. Whisking constantly, slowly drizzle in oil. Add cucumber-tomato mixture, chickpeas, olives, onion, and parsley and toss to coat. Let sit for at least 5 minutes or up to 20 minutes.
3. Add lettuce and feta and gently toss to combine. Season with salt and pepper to taste.

SHAVED MUSHROOM AND CELERY SALAD

INGREDIENTS FOR 6 SERVINGS:

- ¼ cup extra-virgin olive oil
- 1½ tbsp. lemon juice
- Salt and pepper
- 8 ounces cremini mushrooms, trimmed and sliced thin
- 1 shallot, halved and sliced thin
- 4 celery ribs, sliced thin, plus ½ cup celery leaves
- 2 ounces Parmesan cheese, shaved
- ½ cup fresh parsley leaves
- 2 tbsp. chopped fresh tarragon

DIRECTIONS:

1. 1. Whisk oil, lemon juice, and ¼ tsp. salt together in large bowl. Add mushrooms and shallot, toss to coat, and let sit for 10 minutes.
2. 2. Add sliced celery and leaves, Parmesan, parsley, and tarragon to mushroom-shallot mixture and toss to combine. Season with salt and pepper to taste.

CLASSIC HUMMUS

 INGREDIENTS FOR ABOUT 2 CUPS:

- ¼ cup water
- 3 tbsp. lemon juice
- 6 tbsp. tahini
- 2 tbsp. extra-virgin olive oil, plus extra for serving
- 1 (15-ounce) can chickpeas, rinsed
- 1 small garlic clove, minced
- ½ tsp. salt
- ¼ tsp. ground cumin
- Pinch cayenne pepper

DIRECTIONS:

1. Combine water and lemon juice in small bowl. In separate bowl, whisk tahini and oil together.
2. Process chickpeas, garlic, salt, cumin, and cayenne in food processor until almost fully ground, about 15 seconds. Scrape down sides of bowl with rubber spatula. With machine running, add lemon juice mixture in steady stream. Scrape down sides of bowl and continue to process for 1 minute. With machine running, add tahini mixture in steady stream and process until hummus is smooth and creamy, about 15 seconds, scraping down sides of bowl as needed.
3. Transfer hummus to serving bowl, cover with plastic wrap, and let sit at room temperature until flavors meld, about 30 minutes. (Hummus can be refrigerated for up to 5 days; if necessary, loosen hummus with 1 tbsp. warm water before serving.) Drizzle with extra oil to taste before serving.

MUHAMMARA

 INGREDIENTS FOR ABOUT 2 CUPS:

- 1½ cups jarred roasted red peppers, rinsed and patted dry
- 1 cup walnuts, toasted
- ¼ cup plain wheat crackers, crumbled
- 3 tbsp. pomegranate molasses
- 2 tbsp. extra-virgin olive oil
- ¾ tsp. salt
- ½ tsp. ground cumin
- tsp. cayenne pepper
- Lemon juice, as needed
- 1 tbsp. minced fresh parsley (optional)

 DIRECTIONS:

1. Pulse all ingredients except parsley in food processor until smooth, about 10 pulses. Transfer to serving bowl, cover, and refrigerate for 15 minutes. (Dip can be refrigerated for up to 24 hours; bring to room temperature before serving.) Season with lemon juice, salt, and cayenne to taste and sprinkle with parsley, if using, before serving.

MARINATED ARTICHOKES

 INGREDIENTS FOR 6 SERVINGS:

- 2 lemons
- 2½ cups extra-virgin olive oil
- 3 pounds baby artichokes (2 to 4 ounces each)
- 8 garlic cloves, peeled, 6 cloves smashed, 2 cloves minced
- ¼ tsp. red pepper lakes
- 2 sprigs fresh thyme
- Salt and pepper
- 2 tbsp. minced fresh mint

 DIRECTIONS:

1. Using vegetable peeler, remove three 2-inch strips zest from 1 lemon. Grate ½ tsp. zest from second lemon and set aside. Halve and juice lemons to yield ¼ cup juice, reserving spent lemon halves.
2. Combine oil and lemon zest strips in large saucepan. Working with 1 artichoke at a time, cut top quarter of each artichoke, snap of outer leaves, and trim away dark parts. Peel and trim stem, then cut artichoke in half lengthwise (quarter artichoke if large). Rub each artichoke half with spent lemon half and place in saucepan.
3. Add smashed garlic, pepper flakes, thyme sprigs, 1 tsp. salt, and ¼ tsp. pepper to saucepan and bring to rapid simmer over high heat. Reduce heat to medium-low and simmer, stirring occasionally to submerge all artichokes, until artichokes can be pierced with fork but are still firm, about 5 minutes. Remove from heat, cover, and let sit until artichokes are fork-tender and fully cooked, about 20 minutes.
4. Gently stir in ½ tsp. reserved grated lemon zest, ¼ cup reserved lemon juice, and minced garlic. Transfer artichokes and oil to serving bowl and let cool to room temperature. Season with salt to taste and sprinkle with mint. (Artichokes and oil can be refrigerated for up to 4 days.)

MUSSELS ESCABÈCHE

 INGREDIENTS FOR 6 SERVINGS:

- 2/3 cup white wine
- 2/3 cup water
- 2 pounds mussels, scrubbed and debearded
- ⅓ cup extra-virgin olive oil
- ½ small red onion, sliced ¼ inch thick
- 4 garlic cloves, sliced thin
- 2 bay leaves
- 2 sprigs fresh thyme
- 2 tbsp. minced fresh parsley
- ¾ tsp. smoked paprika
- ¼ cup sherry vinegar
- Salt and pepper

 DIRECTIONS:

1. Bring wine and water to boil in Dutch oven over high heat. Add mussels, cover, and cook, stirring occasionally, until mussels open, 3 to 6 minutes. Strain mussels and discard cooking liquid and any mussels that have not opened. Let mussels cool slightly, then remove mussels from shells and place in large bowl; discard shells.
2. Heat oil in now-empty Dutch oven over medium heat until shimmering. Add onion, garlic, bay leaves, thyme, 1 tbsp. parsley, and paprika. Cook, stirring often, until garlic is fragrant and onion is slightly wilted, about 1 minute.
3. Of heat, stir in vinegar, ¼ tsp. salt, and ½ tsp. pepper. Pour mixture over mussels and let sit for 15 minutes. (Mussels can be refrigerated for up to 2 days; bring to room temperature before serving.) Season with salt and pepper to taste and sprinkle with remaining 1 tbsp. parsley before serving.

YOGURT-TOPPED SQUASH FRITTERS

 INGREDIENTS FOR 4 SERVINGS:

- 6 small yellow squash, grated
- 1 ¼ tsp. Himalayan salt (divided)
- ½ lemon, juiced
- 2 tsp. sweet smoked paprika
- 1 cup plain Greek yogurt
- ¼ tsp. white pepper
- ½ cup all-purpose flour
- 3 large free-range eggs, beaten
- 4 spring onions, thinly sliced
- ¼ cup fresh parsley, finely chopped
- 4 oz. feta cheese, crumbled
- olive oil for frying

 DIRECTIONS:

1. Toss the grated squash in a large bowl with 1 tsp. of salt. Transfer to a colander set over the sink, and allow to drain for at least 20 minutes. Use the back of a wooden spoon or ladle to gently press any excess water from the vegetables, before transferring them back to a bowl.
2. In a small glass bowl, whisk together the lemon juice, paprika, yogurt, and ¼ tsp. of salt. Set aside.
3. Add the pepper, flour, eggs, spring onions, parsley, and crumbled feta to the bowl with the squash, gently stirring to combine.
4. In a large frying pan over medium-high heat, heat ½-inch of oil. Test the oil by inserting the tip of a toothpick – the oil is ready when the toothpick immediately begins to sizzle. Use a ladle to carefully drop the batter into the hot oil – about 4-5 fritters at a time. Lightly flatten the fritters with a spatula, and fry for 2 minutes. Flip, and fry the other side for an additional 2 minutes, or until both sides are lightly browned.
5. Transfer the cooked fritters to a serving platter, and keep warm.
6. Serve the fritters warm, topped with the yogurt dressing.

ZESTY WHITE WINE MARINATED OLIVES

 INGREDIENTS FOR 4 SERVINGS:

- ½ tsp. cayenne pepper
- 4 tsp. crushed garlic
- 3 tbsp. no-salt-added seasoning blend
- ¼ cup sunflower oil
- ½ cup white wine
- 3 tbsp. orange juice
- 3 tbsp. lime juice
- 3 tbsp. lemon juice
- 2 tsp. finely grated orange zest
- 2 tsp. finely grated lime zest
- 2 tsp. finely grated lemon zest
- 4 cups mixed pitted olives

 DIRECTIONS:

1. In a large bowl, whisk together the cayenne pepper, garlic, seasoning blend, sunflower oil, and wine. Whisk in the orange juice, lime juice, lemon juice, orange zest, lime zest, and lemon zest.
2. Gently stir in the olives. Cover the bowl, and chill for a minimum of 4 hours before serving.

TOASTED BREAD FOR BRUSCHETTA

 INGREDIENTS FOR 4 SERVINGS:

- 1 (10 by 5-inch) loaf country bread with thick crust, ends discarded, sliced crosswise into ¾ -inch-thick pieces
- 1 garlic clove, peeled
- Extra-virgin olive oil
- Salt

DIRECTIONS:

1. Adjust oven rack 4 inches from broiler element and heat broiler. Place bread on aluminum foil – lined baking sheet. Broil until bread is deep golden and toasted on both sides, 1 to 2 minutes per side. Lightly rub 1 side of each toast with garlic (you will not use all of garlic). Brush with oil and season with salt to taste.

OLIVE-STUFFED CHICKEN BREASTS

 INGREDIENTS FOR 4 SERVINGS:

- 2 tbsp. balsamic vinegar
- 1 tbsp. extra-virgin olive oil
- 4 tsp. crushed garlic
- ¼ cup roasted sweet red peppers, drained
- 4 green olives, pitted
- 4 Spanish olives, pitted
- 4 black olives
- 4 oil-packed sun-dried tomatoes
- 4 boneless chicken breasts, skins removed
- Grated Parmesan cheese, for garnishing

DIRECTIONS:

1. In a blender, pulse the vinegar, oil, garlic, sweet peppers, olives, and tomatoes on medium, until you have a lumpy paste.
2. Slice the chicken breasts open, taking care not to cut all the way through. Divide the olive paste between the breasts and use a spoon to fill each one.
3. Spear the breasts closed with toothpicks to ensure that none of the filling escapes.
4. Place the stuffed breasts on a lightly coated rack, and broil in the oven on high for 8- 10 minutes, or until the chicken is properly cooked. Keep an eye on the chicken to ensure it doesn't burn.
5. Remove the toothpicks and serve hot, garnished with the cheese.

CREAMY TURKISH NUT DIP

 INGREDIENTS FOR ABOUT 1 CUP:

- 1 slice hearty white sandwich bread, crusts removed, torn into 1-inch pieces ¾ cup water, plus extra as needed
- 1 cup blanched almonds, blanched hazelnuts, pine nuts, or walnuts, toasted ¼ cup extra-virgin olive oil
- 2 tbsp. lemon juice, plus extra as needed
- 1 small garlic clove, minced
- Salt and pepper
- Pinch cayenne pepper

DIRECTIONS:

1. With fork, mash bread and water together in bowl into paste. Process bread mixture, nuts, oil, lemon juice, garlic, ½ tsp. salt, ⅛ tsp. pepper, and cayenne in blender until smooth, about 2 minutes. Add extra water as needed until sauce is barely thicker than consistency of heavy cream.
2. Season with salt, pepper, and extra lemon juice to taste. Serve at room temperature. (Sauce can be refrigerated for up to 2 days; bring to room temperature before serving.)

YOGURT CHEESE

 INGREDIENTS FOR ABOUT 1 CUP:

- 2 cups plain yogurt

 DIRECTIONS:

1. Line fine-mesh strainer with 3 basket-style cofee filters or double layer of cheesecloth. Set strainer over large measuring cup or bowl (there should be enough room for about 1 cup liquid to drain without touching strainer).
2. Spoon yogurt into strainer, cover tightly with plastic wrap, and refrigerate until yogurt has released about 1 cup liquid and has creamy, cream cheese–like texture, at least 10 hours or up to 2 days.
3. Transfer drained yogurt to clean container; discard liquid. Serve. (Yogurt can be refrigerated for up to 2 days.)

BRUSCHETTA WITH ARTICHOKE HEARTS AND PARMESAN

 INGREDIENTS FOR 4 SERVINGS:

- 1 cup jarred whole baby artichoke hearts packed in water, rinsed and patted dry
- 2 tbsp. extra-virgin olive oil, plus extra for serving
- 2 tbsp. chopped fresh basil
- 2 tsp. lemon juice
- 1 garlic clove, minced
- Salt and pepper
- 2 ounces Parmesan cheese, 1 ounce grated ine, 1 ounce shaved 1 recipe Toasted Bread for Bruschetta

 DIRECTIONS:

1. Pulse artichoke hearts, oil, basil, lemon juice, garlic, ¼ tsp. salt, and ¼ tsp. pepper in food processor until coarsely pu-reed, about 6 pulses, scraping down sides of bowl as needed. Add grated Parmesan and pulse to combine, about 2 pulses. Spread artichoke mixture evenly on toasts and top with shaved Parmesan. Season with pepper to taste, and drizzle with extra oil to taste.

RAINBOW TROUT HERB PATE

 INGREDIENTS FOR 6 SERVINGS:

- 2 tsp. fresh parsley, finely chopped
- ⅛ tsp. white pepper
- 1 tbsp. lime juice
- 1 tbsp. horseradish sauce
- ½ cup half-and-half cream

- 3 oz. reduced-fat cream cheese
- 1 lb. flaked smoked rainbow trout
- 16 cucumber slices
- 16 assorted crackers

 DIRECTIONS:

1. In a food processor, pulse the parsley, pepper, lime juice, horseradish sauce, cream, cream cheese, and trout on high, until you have a smooth paste.
2. Arrange the 16 crackers on a serving platter, and top each with a thin slice of cucumber. Place about 1 tsp. of pate onto each cucumber slice, and serve.

SKORDALIA

 INGREDIENTS FOR ABOUT 2 CUPS:

- 1 (10- to 12-ounce) russet potato, peeled and cut into 1-inch chunks 3 garlic cloves, minced to paste
- 3 tbsp. lemon juice
- 2 slices hearty white sandwich bread, crusts removed, torn into 1-inch pieces
- 6 tbsp. warm water, plus extra as needed
- Salt and pepper
- ¼ cup extra-virgin olive oil
- ¼ cup plain Greek yogurt

DIRECTIONS:

1. Place potato in small saucepan and add water to cover by 1 inch. Bring water to boil, then reduce to simmer and cook until potato is tender and paring knife can be inserted into potato with no resistance, 15 to 20 minutes. Drain potato in colander, tossing to remove any excess water.
2. Meanwhile, combine garlic and lemon juice in bowl and let sit for 10 minutes. In separate medium bowl, mash bread, ¼ cup warm water, and ½ tsp. salt into paste with fork.
3. Transfer potato to ricer (food mill fitted with small disk) and process into bowl with bread mixture. Stir in lemon-garlic mixture, oil, yogurt, and remaining 2 tbsp. warm water until well combined. (Sauce can be refrigerated for up to 3 days; bring to room temperature before serving.) Season with salt and pepper to taste and adjust consistency with extra warm water as needed before serving.

STUFFED SARDINES

 INGREDIENTS FOR 4 SERVINGS:

- ⅓ cup capers, rinsed and minced
- ¼ cup golden raisins, chopped ine
- ¼ cup pine nuts, toasted and chopped ine
- 3 tbsp. extra-virgin olive oil
- 2 tbsp. minced fresh parsley
- 2 tsp. grated orange zest plus wedges for serving

- 2 garlic cloves, minced
- Salt and pepper
- ⅓ cup panko bread crumbs
- 8 fresh sardines (2 to 3 ounces each), scaled, gutted, head and tail on

DIRECTIONS:

1. Adjust oven rack to lower-middle position and heat oven to 450 degrees. Line rimmed baking sheet with aluminum foil. Combine capers, raisins, pine nuts, 1 tbsp. oil, parsley, orange zest, garlic, 1/4 tsp. salt, and ¼ tsp. pepper in bowl. Add panko and gently stir to combine.
2. Using paring knife, slit belly of fish open from gill to tail, leaving spine intact. Gently rinse fish under cold running water and pat dry with paper towels. Rub skin of sardines evenly with remaining 2 tbsp. oil and season with salt and pepper.
3. Place sardines on prepared sheet, spaced 1 inch apart. Stu cavities of each sardine with 2 tbsp. filling and press on filling to help it adhere; gently press fish closed.
4. Bake until fish flakes apart when gently prodded with paring knife and filling is golden brown, about 15 minutes. Serve with orange wedges.

CHAPTER 10: DESSERTS/FRUITS/CANDIE

TURKISH STUFFED APRICOTS WITH ROSE WATER AND PISTACHIOS

 INGREDIENTS FOR 6 SERVINGS:

- ½ cup plain Greek yogurt
- ¼ cup sugar
- ½ tsp. rose water
- ½ tsp. grated lemon zest plus 1 tbsp. juice
- Salt
- 2 cups water
- 4 green cardamom pods, cracked
- 2 bay leaves
- 24 whole dried apricots
- ¼ cup shelled pistachios, toasted and chopped ine

DIRECTIONS:

1. Combine yogurt, 1 tsp. sugar, rose water, lemon zest, and pinch salt in small bowl. Refrigerate filling until ready to use.
2. Bring water, cardamom pods, bay leaves, lemon juice, and remaining sugar to simmer in small saucepan over medium-low heat and cook, stirring occasionally, until sugar has dissolved, about 2 minutes. Stir in apricots, return to simmer, and cook, stirring occasionally, until plump and tender, 25 to 30 minutes. Using slotted spoon, transfer apricots to plate and let cool to room temperature.
3. Discard cardamom pods and bay leaves. Bring syrup to boil over high heat and cook, stirring occasionally, until thickened and measures about 3 tbsp., 4 to 6 minutes; let cool to room temperature.
4. Place pistachios in shallow dish. Place filling in small zipper-lock bag and snip of 1 corner to create ½-inch opening. Pipe filling evenly into opening of each apricot and dip exposed filling into pistachios; transfer to serving platter. Drizzle apricots with syrup and serve.

STRAWBERRIES WITH BALSAMIC VINEGAR

 INGREDIENTS FOR 6 SERVINGS:

- ⅓ cup balsamic vinegar
- 2 tsp. granulated sugar
- ½ tsp. lemon juice
- 2 pounds strawberries, hulled and sliced lengthwise ¼ inch thick (5 cups) ¼ cup packed light brown sugar
- Pinch pepper

 DIRECTIONS:

1. Bring vinegar, granulated sugar, and lemon juice to simmer in small saucepan over medium heat and cook, stirring occasionally, until thickened and measures about 3 tbsp., about 3 minutes. Transfer syrup to small bowl and let cool completely.
2. Gently toss strawberries with brown sugar and pepper in large bowl. Let sit at room temperature, stirring occasionally, until strawberries begin to release their juice, 10 to 15 minutes. Pour syrup over strawberries and gently toss to combine.

SPICED BISCOTTI

 INGREDIENTS FOR ABOUT 48 BISCOTTI:

- 2¼ cups (11¼ ounces) all-purpose lour
- 1 tsp. baking powder
- ½ tsp. baking soda
- ½ tsp. ground cloves
- ½ tsp. ground cinnamon
- ¼ tsp. ground ginger
- ¼ tsp. salt
- ¼ tsp. ground white pepper
- 1 cup (7 ounces) sugar
- 2 large eggs plus 2 large yolks
- ½ tsp. vanilla extract

DIRECTIONS:

1. Adjust oven rack to middle position and heat oven to 350 degrees. Using ruler and pencil, draw two 13 by 2-inch rectangles, spaced 3 inches apart, on piece of parchment paper. Grease baking sheet and place parchment on it, marked side down.
2. Whisk flour, baking powder, baking soda, cloves, cinnamon, ginger, salt, and pepper together in small bowl. In large bowl, whisk sugar and eggs and egg yolks together until pale yellow. Whisk in vanilla until combined. Using rubber spatula, stir in flour mixture until just combined.
3. Divide dough in half. Using floured hands, form each half into 13 by 2- inch rectangle, using lines on parchment as guide. Using rubber spatula lightly coated with vegetable oil spray, smooth tops and sides of loaves. Bake until loaves are golden and just beginning to crack on top, about 35 minutes, rotating sheet halfway through baking.
4. Let loaves cool on sheet for 10 minutes, then transfer to cutting board. Reduce oven temperature to 325 degrees. Using serrated knife, slice each loaf on slight bias into ½-inch-thick slices.
5. Arrange cookies cut side down on sheet about ½ inch apart and bake until crisp and golden brown on both sides, about 15 minutes, flipping cookies halfway through baking. Let cool completely on wire rack before serving. (Biscotti can be stored at room temperature for up to 1 month.)

OLIVE OIL-YOGURT CAKE

 INGREDIENTS FOR 12 SERVINGS:

CAKE
- 3 cups (15 ounces) all-purpose lour
- 1 tbsp. baking powder
- 1 tsp. salt
- 1¼ cups (8¾ ounces) granulated sugar
- 4 large eggs
- 1¼ cups extra-virgin olive oil
- 1 cup plain whole-milk yogurt

LEMON GLAZE
- 2 - 3 tbsp. lemon juice
- 1 tbsp. plain whole-milk yogurt
- 2 cups (8 ounces) confectioners' sugar

 DIRECTIONS:

1. FOR THE CAKE Adjust oven rack to lower-middle position and heat oven to 350 degrees. Grease 12-cup nonstick Bundt pan. Whisk flour, baking powder, and salt together in bowl. In separate large bowl, whisk sugar and eggs together until sugar is mostly dissolved and mixture is pale and frothy, about 1 minute. Whisk in oil and yogurt until combined. Using rubber spatula, stir in flour mixture until combined and no dry flour remains.
2. Pour batter into prepared pan, smooth top, and gently tap pan on counter to settle batter. Bake until cake is golden brown and wooden skewer inserted into center comes out clean, 40 to 45 minutes, rotating pan halfway through baking.
3. FOR THE LEMON GLAZE Whisk 2 tbsp. lemon juice, yogurt, and confectioners' sugar together in bowl until smooth, adding more lemon juice gradually as needed until glaze is thick but still pourable (mixture should leave faint trail across bottom of mixing bowl when drizzled from whisk). Let cake cool in pan for 10 minutes, then gently turn cake out onto wire rack. Drizzle half of glaze over warm cake and let cool for 1 hour. Drizzle remaining glaze over cake and let cool completely, about 2 hours.

DARK CHOCOLATE HAZELNUT TRUFFLES

 INGREDIENTS FOR 6 SERVINGS:

- 1 ¾ cups blanched hazelnuts (divided)
- low-carb sweetener to taste (optional)
- 1 tsp. ground cinnamon
- ¼ tsp. ground nutmeg
- ¼ cup cocoa powder
- ¼ cup collagen powder
- 4 tbsp. unsalted butter
- ½ cup coconut butter
- 1 oz. cocoa butter
- 2 ½ oz. dark dairy milk chocolate, chopped

 DIRECTIONS:

1. Set the oven to preheat to 285°F, with the wire rack in the center of the oven. Cover a large baking tray with greaseproof paper.
2. Fan the hazelnuts out over a clean baking tray. Dry roast the nuts in the oven for 40- 50 minutes, until nicely toasted. Cool on the counter while you prepare the rest of the dish.
3. Transfer 1 cup of the roasted hazelnuts to a blender, and pulse a few times. You want an almost fine, chunky mixture. Add the optional sweetener, cinnamon, nutmeg, cocoa, collagen, unsalted butter, and coconut butter to the blender, and pulse until the ingredients come together to form a dough. Gather the dough into a smooth ball, and cover in cling wrap before chilling for 1 hour.
4. Remove 12 hazelnuts from the pan, and set aside. Crumble the rest of the nuts into a large mixing bowl.
5. Place the cocoa butter and dark chocolate in a glass bowl. Microwave on high for about 1 ½ minutes, stirring every 30 seconds until the chocolate is completely melted.
6. Once the dough is nicely chilled, form the mixture into 12 truffles of roughly the same size. Press one of the reserved hazelnuts into the center of each truffle. Cover the hazelnuts in the center of each truffle, and smooth out the surface. Place the 12 truffles on the prepared baking tray, and place the tray in the freezer for 15 minutes.
7. Gently spear each chilled truffle with a toothpick. Hold each truffle over the bowl of melted chocolate, and spoon the mixture over the ball while turning the toothpick to coat the ball. The chocolate will harden quickly, so immediately roll the coated truffle in the chopped hazelnuts. Return the coated truffle to the pan. Repeat the process with the remaining truffles. Drizzle any remaining chocolate and nuts over all of the truffles. Serve and enjoy.

LEMON SHERBET

 INGREDIENTS FOR 4 SERVINGS:

- 2 egg whites
- 200 g granulated sugar
- 100 ml white wine
- The juice of 4 lemons
- 4 cl vodka
- The zest of a lemon

DIRECTIONS:

1. Rub the zest of the lemon. Squeeze the juice out of the four lemons. Boil 400 ml of water with the lemon zest and the sugar.
2. Add the wine, lemon juice and vodka and freeze in an ice maker.
3. Beat the egg white with sugar and stir into the sherbet before serving.

EGG AND LIME CREAM

INGREDIENTS FOR 1 SERVING:

- 80 g of sugar
- 3 limes
- 45 g butter
- 2 eggs

DIRECTIONS:

1. Wash the limes hot. Rub the peel and squeeze the lime. Cut the butter into pieces. Beat the eggs with the sugar in a water bath until frothy.
2. Add the lime juice and the lime zest and stir until it has a creamy consistency. Put the butter pieces in the cream and melt in it.
3. Let the cream cool and store in the refrigerator.

WARM FIGS WITH GOAT CHEESE AND HONEY

INGREDIENTS FOR 6 SERVINGS:

- 1½ ounces goat cheese
- 8 fresh igs, halved lengthwise
- 16 walnut halves, toasted
- 3 tbsp. honey

DIRECTIONS:

1. Adjust oven rack to middle position and heat oven to 500 degrees. Spoon heaping ½ tsp. goat cheese onto each fig half and arrange in parchment paper–lined rimmed baking sheet. Bake figs until heated through, about 4 minutes; transfer to serving platter.
2. Place 1 walnut half on top of each fig half and drizzle with honey.

LEMON ICE

INGREDIENTS FOR 8 SERVINGS:

- 2¼ cups water, preferably spring water
- 1 cup lemon juice (6 lemons)
- 1 cup (7 ounces) sugar
- 2 tbsp. vodka (optional)
- ⅛ tsp. salt

DIRECTIONS:

1. Whisk all ingredients together in bowl until sugar has dissolved. Pour mixture into 2 ice cube trays and freeze until solid, at least 3 hours or up to 5 days.
2. Place medium bowl in freezer. Pulse half of ice cubes in food processor until creamy and no large lumps remain, about 18 pulses. Transfer mixture to chilled bowl and return to freezer. Repeat pulsing remaining ice cubes; transfer to bowl. Serve immediately.

DECADENT EGGLESS CHOCOLATE MOUSSE

 INGREDIENTS FOR 4 SERVINGS:

- 1 cup dark dairy milk chocolate, chopped
- ⅓ tsp. kosher salt
- ½ tsp. pure vanilla essence
- 2 tsp. full-cream milk

- 2 tbsp. dark brown sugar (divided)
- ½ cup aquafaba at room temperature
- ½ tsp. cream of tartar
- Lightly toasted walnuts, chopped

 DIRECTIONS:

1. Place the chopped chocolate in a glass bowl over a pot of boiling water. The water should not be touching the bottom of the bowl. Gently stir the chocolate as it melts. When the chocolate is completely smooth, transfer the bowl to a wooden chopping board.
2. Add the salt, vanilla, milk, and half of the sugar to the melted chocolate, stirring to combine.
3. Place the aquafaba in the large bowl of a stand mixer, and beat on high for about 1 minute, until light and bubbly. Gently beat in the cream of tartar, until the mixture resembles a cloud. Beat in the remaining sugar, until the cloud forms stiff peaks.
4. Working in about 3 or 4 batches, add the fluffy aquafaba to the melted chocolate, and use an offset spatula to gently fold the ingredients together. You want to be as gentle as possible.
5. Once all of the aquafaba has been folded into the melted chocolate, scoop the mixture into 4 glass bowls. Refrigerate covered for a few hours.
6. When the mousse is properly chilled, sprinkle with the walnuts, and serve.

DECADENTLY SIMPLE CHOCOLATE PUDDING

 INGREDIENTS FOR 4 SERVINGS:

- ⅛ tsp. kosher salt
- 2 tbsp. pure cocoa powder
- 2 tbsp. dark brown sugar

- 3 tbsp. corn flour
- 2 cups almond milk
- 1 tsp. pure vanilla essence

DIRECTIONS:

1.1 DIn a small pot, whisk together the salt, cocoa powder, sugar, and corn flour. Whisk in the milk, and whisk the mixture over medium heat until the pudding begins to bubble. Once the pudding is bubbling, lower the heat to low, and gently whisk for an additional 2 minutes.
2.2 DTransfer the pot to a wooden chopping board, and whisk in the vanilla. Leave the pot on the counter to cool,
3.3 Dstirring at regular intervals to prevent a crust from forming. The cooling process should take about 15 minutes.
4.4 DScoop the pudding into serving bowls, and cover the bowls with cling wrap. Chill the pudding for a minimum of 30 minutes before serving.

BRUNCH MUFFINS WITH FIGS

 INGREDIENTS FOR 6 SERVINGS:

- 2 tbsp. melted butter
- 2 cups of brunch
- 6 figs
- 4 tbsp. orange liqueur

- 4 tbsp. liquid honey
- ½ tsp. cinnamon
- 125 g of sugar
- 3 eggs

 DIRECTIONS:

1. Wash the figs and cut them in half.
2. Drizzle the honey over the figs and marinate in them. Beat the eggs with the brunch, orange liqueur, cinnamon and 1 tbsp. melted butter to a cream. Preheat the oven to 180 ° C top / bottom heat. Place muffin cups in a muffin tin. Pour in the brunch cream and fill with a fig. Put the rest of the butter on top.
3. Bake the muffins for 20-25 minutes.

WILD BERRIES WITH ICE

INGREDIENTS FOR 6 SERVINGS:

- 500 g
- 5 egg yolks
- 250 ml whipped cream

- 120 g of sugar
- 1 vanilla stick
- 250 ml milk

DIRECTIONS:

1. Mix the egg yolks into a cream. Gradually add sugar.
2. Bring the milk to the boil and soak the vanilla stick. Then cut open the vanilla stick and take out the pulp. Stir the vanilla pulp into the hot milk. Add the milk to the egg yolk cream and heat, stirring constantly. Bring everything to the boil and then let it cool down. Whip the whipped cream until stiff and freeze everything. Arrange the wild berries on a plate with the ice cream.

PEACH COBBLER WITH A TWIST

INGREDIENTS FOR 8 SERVINGS:

- ½ tsp. finely grated lime zest
- 2 tsp. ground cinnamon
- 4 tsp. corn flour
- 2 tbsp. minced crystallized ginger
- 3 tbsp. fine white sugar
- 1 tbsp. freshly squeezed lime juice
- 8 medium peaches, peeled and sliced
- ¼ cup dark brown packed sugar (plus 2 tbsp.)

- 3 tbsp. unsalted butter, softened
- 1 cup all-purpose flour
- ¼ tsp. kosher salt
- ½ tsp. baking powder
- 2 tbsp. cold water
- ¼ cup chopped pecans
- 2 tbsp. buttermilk
- Yolk of 1 large egg

DIRECTIONS:

1. Set the oven to preheat to 375°F, with the wire rack in the center of the oven. Lightly coat a large casserole dish with baking spray.
2. In a large mixing bowl, whisk together the lime zest, cinnamon, corn flour, crystallized ginger, and sugar. Stir in the lime juice and sliced peaches until all of the ingredients are properly combined. Scrape the mixture into the prepared casserole dish in an even layer.
3. In a clean mixing bowl, whisk the ¼ cup dark brown sugar and butter together, until light and fluffy. In a separate bowl, whisk together the remaining 2 tbsp. of sugar, all-purpose flour, salt, and baking powder. Add the flour mixture to the butter and sugar, beating until properly combined. Stir in the water until the mixture begins to crumble. Fold in the chopped pecans. Crumble and strew the mixture over the filling in the casserole dish.
4. In a small glass bowl, whisk together the buttermilk and egg yolk. Carefully drizzle the egg mixture over everything in the casserole dish.
5. Place the dish in the oven, and bake for 35-40 minutes, or until the crumble topping is nicely toasted.
6. Serve the cobbler warm with a topping of your choice, such as vanilla ice cream or whipped cream.

PICKLED PEARS WITH VANILLA ICE CREAM

INGREDIENTS FOR 4 SERVINGS:

- 8 mint leaves
- 4 pears
- 160 g vanilla ice cream
- 80 g granulated sugar
- 3 cloves
- 1 packet of vanilla sugar

- ½ stick of cinnamon
- 500 ml red wine
- 1 vanilla pod
- 100 ml blackberry liqueur
- The juice of one lemon

DIRECTIONS:

1. Halve the vanilla pod and scrape out the pulp. Squeeze the lemon.
2. Bring the red wine to the boil with the sugar, vanilla sugar, lemon juice, vanilla pod, blackberry liqueur, vanilla pulp, cinnamon stick and cloves.
3. Place the pears in it and let steep for 25 minutes, turning occasionally. Let the whole thing cool and let it steep in the fridge overnight.
4. Then halve and core the pears. Pour vanilla ice cream into the hollow and garnish with the mint leaves.

APPENDIX 1: SHOPPING LIST

When going shopping, choose nutrient-rich foods like fruits, vegetables, nuts, seeds, legumes, and whole grains. Here are some essential items of the Mediterranean diet to include in your shopping list.

	Vegetables:	Carrots, onions, broccoli, spinach, kale, garlic, zucchini, and mushrooms
	Frozen veggies:	Peas, carrots, broccoli, and mixed vegetables
	Tubers:	Potatoes, sweet potatoes, and yams
	Fruits:	Apples, bananas, oranges, grapes, melons, peaches, pears, strawberries, and blueberries
	Grains:	Whole grain bread, whole grain pasta, quinoa, brown rice, and oats
	Legumes:	Lentils, chickpeas, black beans, and kidney beans
	Nuts:	Almonds, walnuts, cashews, pistachios, and macadamia nuts
	Seeds:	Sunflower seeds, pumpkin seeds, chia seeds, and hemp seeds
	Dairy products:	Greek yogurt, yogurt, and milk
	Seafood:	Salmon, sardines, mackerel, trout, shrimp, and mussels
	Poultry:	Chicken, duck, and turkey
	Eggs:	Chicken, quail, and duck eggs
	Healthy fats:	Extra virgin olive oil, olives, avocados, and avocado oil
	Condiments:	Sea salt, pepper, turmeric, cinnamon, cayenne pepper, and oregano

APPENDIX 2: THE DIRTY DOZEN AND CLEAN FIFTEEN

"The Dirty Dozen and Clean Fifteen" is a list released annually by the Environmental Working Group (EWG) in the United States.

"The Dirty Dozen" refers to 12 types of fruits and vegetables that are more severely contaminated by pesticide residues. They usually include strawberries, spinach, kale, nectarines, apples, grapes, peaches, cherries, pears, tomatoes, celery, and potatoes.

"The Clean Fifteen" are 15 types of fruits and vegetables with relatively less pesticide residues. Commonly, they are avocados, sweet corn, pineapples, onions, papayas, sweet peas (frozen), eggplants, asparagus, broccoli, cauliflower, cantaloupes, kiwis, cabbages, honeydew melons, and bananas.

It should be noted that this list by the EWG is based on its own testing and assessment methods. Different regions, planting methods, and testing means may lead to varying results. In daily life, regardless of which fruits and vegetables are consumed, thorough washing can help reduce pesticide residues.

Washing fruits and vegetables to remove pesticide residues can be done in several effective ways:

Simple Rinse with Water: Wash the produce under running tap water. For items with a rough surface like cucumbers or melons, use a brush to gently scrub.
Example: Rinse apples under running water for a minute or two to remove surface dirt and some pesticide residue.

Soaking in Water: Soak the fruits and vegetables in a bowl of water for 10-15 minutes. This can help loosen and dissolve some residues.
For instance, soaking leafy greens like spinach or kale can be beneficial.

Vinegar Solution: Make a mixture of water and vinegar (about 3 parts water to 1 part vinegar) and soak the produce in it for a few minutes. Then rinse thoroughly with water.
An example could be soaking strawberries in the vinegar solution to remove impurities.

Baking Soda Solution: Prepare a solution of water and baking soda (a teaspoon of baking soda per litre of water) and soak the produce for 15 minutes before rinsing.
This method can be used for items like grapes.

Peeling: For fruits and vegetables with a peel that is not eaten, such as bananas, oranges, or melons, peeling can remove most of the pesticide residue.
However, note that some nutrients may also be lost when peeling.
It's important to wash fruits and vegetables thoroughly before eating or cooking to minimize the potential exposure to pesticide residues and ensure their safety.

APPENDIX 3:
KITCHEN MEASUREMENT
CANVERSION CHART

MEASUREMENT CONVERSION CHART

VOLUME EQUIVALENTS(DRY)

US STANDARD	METRIC (APPROXIM ATE)
1/8 teaspoon	0.5 mL
1/4 teaspoon	1 mL
1/2 teaspoon	2 mL
3/4 teaspoon	4 mL
1 teaspoon	5 mL
1 tablespoon	15 mL
1 tablespoon	59 mL
1/2 cup	118 mL
3/4 cup	177 mL
1 cup	235 mL
2 cups	475 mL
3 cups	700 mL
4 cups	1L

VOLUME EQUIVALENTS(LIQUID)

US STANDARD	US STANDARD (OUNCES)	METRIC (APPROXIMATE)
2 tablespoons	1 fl.oz.	30 mL
1/4 cup	2 fl.oz.	60 mL
1/2 cup	4 fl.oz.	120 mL
1 cup	8 fl.oz.	240 mL
1 1/2 cuP	12 fl.oz.	355 mL
2 cups or 1 pint	16 fl.oz.	475 mL
4 cups or 1 quart	32 fl.oz.	1L
1 gallon	128 fl.oz.	4L

TEMPERATURES EQUIVALENTS

FAHRENHEIT(F)	CELSIUS(C)(APPROXIMATE)
225 °F	107 °C
250 °F	120 °C
275 °F	135 °C
300 °F	150 °C
325 °F	160 °C
350 °F	180 °C
375 °F	190 °C
400 °F	205 °C
425 °F	220 °C
450 °F	235 °C
475 °F	245 °C
500 °F	260 °C

WEIGHT EQUIVALENTS

US STANDARD	METRIC (APPROXIM ATE)
1 ounce	28g
2 ounces	57g
5 ounces	142g
10 ounces	284g
15 ounces	425g
16 ounces (1 pound)	455g
1.5 pounds	680 g
2 pounds	907 g

APPENDIX 4: RECIPES INDEX

Made in the USA
Columbia, SC
10 October 2024

44131801R00050